CUTTING
ONE RUN AT A TIME

Happy Cutting!

Dream big

Barbra Schulte

A PRACTICAL GUIDE
TO CUTTING SUCCESS

BARBRA SCHULTE
WITH JULIE WELLS
Foreword by PAUL HANSMA

Cover design by Lee Lee Brazeal, Chappell Hill, Texas

Illustrations by Amy Glasgow, Brenham, TX

Photography by John Brasseaux, Associate Editor
Quarter Horse News, Ft. Worth, TX

Photo on the back cover:
Barbra Schulte and Oakin Uno
courtesy of Suzanne Forrest Photography, Houston, TX

Mentally Tough® is a registered trademark of LGE Sport Science, Inc.
Ideal Performance State℠ is a service mark of LGE Sport Science, Inc.
Unlimited Rider™ is a trademark of Center for Equestrian Performance.

Published by the Center for Equestrian Performance, 2000 South Market Street, Suite 219, Brenham, Texas 77833. Third printing.

ISBN 0-9662585-0-9

Printed by Tops Printing, Inc., Bryan, Texas

To my father and mother, Cletus and Marie Hulling . . .

*Two of your many gifts—the horse and a belief in myself—
have given my life much richness.*

Zane, Tom and Barbra Schulte

ABOUT THE AUTHOR

Barbra Schulte has been involved with horses her entire life. Beginning in early childhood and continuing through college, she helped market and show many of her family's 500 head of horses. She competed in western pleasure, reining, horsemanship, and cutting.

After high school, Barbra went on to gain a master's degree in Speech Pathology and Audiology. In a few short years, she became an administrator at Arizona State School for the Deaf and taught at the University of Arizona in Tucson, Arizona.

In 1983, Barbra's love of horses led her back to the competitive cutting arena, and she embarked on a career as a professional horse trainer. In 1986, after reading *Mental Toughness Training for Sports*, by Dr. James Loehr of LGE Sports Science, Inc., she began to incorporate his training techniques into her own. After combining the performance-enhancing techniques of the Mentally Tough program with her own wealth of experience as a trainer, Barbra began to see remarkable results. She captured the 1988 NCHA Derby, the 1992 NCHA Super Stakes Classic, and the 1992 Augusta Futurity championships—the first woman to wear those crowns. Horses and riders trained by Barbra have earned multiple national and regional titles and championships along the way.

Barbra's philosophy is simple: to perform at their highest levels, both horse and rider must be calm, focused, and understand the task at hand. This is accomplished over time by practicing, examining feedback to determine what aspects are working and which need tuning, practicing more, and then, again, examining the total training program. Improve upon what's working and eliminate what's not.

In 1994, recognizing the powerful benefits of the Mentally Tough program, Schulte significantly expanded her career as an equine professional and began to introduce the Mentally Tough program to riders in all disciplines. She realized in addition to training cutting horses there was another field that intrigued her, as well. She had a deep desire to understand how to teach equestrians to reach peak performance levels, consistently under pressure. She became certified as a Personal Performance Coach by LGE in 1994 and began conducting clinics and seminars throughout the United States, Canada, Australia, and Europe. Today, she is the only person licensed to teach the Mentally Tough concepts to equestrian enthusiasts.

Barbra has developed a wide line of educational products

specifically geared towards riders. She has produced a three-part video series focusing specifically on cutting, a six-part Mentally Tough Riding audio series, and two individual audio cassettes addressing riding and coaching skills. Barbra is frequently a featured speaker at major horse industry events and she is also a syndicated columnist.

Barbra continues to compete in major NCHA aged events, and she conducts clinics and seminars in both the United States and Canada. She is a past vice president of the National Cutting Horse Association and has represented the National Cutting Horse Association on "Good Morning America." She lives in Brenham with her husband, Tom who coaches girl's basketball, judges and shows cutting horses. Their son Zane, passed away in 2000 from bone cancer. The Zane Schulte Award is given annually in his memory by the NCHA to a trainer who exemplifies the character by which Zane is remembered: integrity, service, values, respect of peers, contribution to the industry, and excellence in the arena.

How To Contact The Author

Barbra Schulte offers a variety of services including horse training and showing, clinics, horse purchase consultations, and keynote addresses. Requests for information about these services should be directed to her at the address below. Readers of this book are also encouraged to contact the author with comments and ideas for future editions.

Barbra Schulte
2000 S. Market St. Suite 219
Brenham, TX 77833
979-277-9344
979-277-9271 (fax)
info@barbraschulte.com

From
JULIE WELLS

When I first met Barbra in 1997, I really didn't know much about her except that she was teaching things that many traditionalists thought were pretty extreme. All my competitive life, I had some vague idea that there were underlying things that conspired to influence an event's outcome. But, to be perfectly honest, it was easier to chalked up most of my competitors' success to some skill and a lot of luck. From the very first time I interviewed Barbra and began to give her teachings some thought, I understood what she is sharing with others is real and it works. For anyone who craves any level of success, listen to what she has to say. I guarantee it will change the way you approach competition; and it might even change the way you approach everyday life.

To Barbra, thank you for the opportunity to work with you on this project. Expanding upon traditional teaching methods might have been too daunting a task for anyone else. Thank you for your courage. You are truly an inspiration.

To my parents, thank you for your encouragement. As a child, you never got tired of reading my stories, and your willingness to be my captive audience is greatly appreciated.

To my late husband, Dan, you continue to be my measuring stick. The seeds you planted in my heart continue to bloom, even in your absence, and the goals you worked to achieve have become the motivation that keeps me going.

Julie is a journalist who works as a full-time freelance writer. She regularly contributes to several publications including *Performance Horse, Quarter Horse News, Western Horseman and Barrel Horse News*. In 1998, she authored *The Ultimate Guide to Barrel Racing*, an electonic book for barrel racers. Her entire life has revolved around horses. She grew up riding and training barrel horses and went to college on a rodeo scholarship. In 2000, she rode her first cutter, and the rest, as they say, is history. She lives in Richards, Texas.

ACKNOWLEDGMENTS

Thank you to my many clients and students who have touched my life and made contributions to this book. Without their desire for training, showing, and information—and their faith that I could help them—I would not have shared my ideas on paper.

I wish to express special gratitude to Julie Wells whose manuscript showed remarkable knowledge and sensitivity. To my sister and warmest friend, Tootie Lyons for her support and coordination of everyone involved with this project. To Sharon Henderson for her competence in the layout. To Kimberly Young for her editing. To Kristie Koronka, Lauren Buth, and Linda Niehuus for their support. To Lee Lee Brazael for her watercolor artistry on the cover. To Amy Glasgow for her friendship and illustration expertise, par excellence. To John Brasseaux for his quality photography. To Bob and Nan Kingsley for their hospitality.

To Dr. James E. Loehr and the entire staff at LGE Sport Science in Orlando, Florida for trusting me to accurately share their wisdom of how people grow stronger. I am eternally grateful for the opportunity to experience and share their years of research and work.

To Paul Hansma, my friend, show helper and one whom I admire greatly for his talent, integrity and professionalism . . .

thank you for your contribution of the Foreword.   To all the people who contributed their personal wisdom in quotes found throughout the book: Joe Heim, Dan Lufkin, Mary Jo Milner, Keith Barnett, Sandy Bonelli, Millie Kay Bouget, Kathy Boone, Lindy Burch, Dick Cogdell, Mitch Farris, Phil Feinberg, Dick Gaines, Winston Hansma, Spencer Harden, Bobby Hawkins, James Hooper, Ronnie Nettles, Jack Newton, John Paxton, Gil Porter, Corky Sokol, Gene Suiter, Carole Thorsnes, Kobie Wood, L.H. Wood, Lee Garner, and Helen Groves.

I wish to acknowledge the countless individuals who so generously offered inspiration, ideas, and information throughout my cutting life. As a young girl, Jim Lee, Gayle Borland, Stanley Bush and J.T. Fisher. As a cutting professional, there are many (including those mentioned above who contributed quotes). I acknowledge and thank Kathy Daughn, Bill Freeman, Buster and Sheila Welch, Jody Galyean, Bill Riddle, Terry Riddle, Lloyd Cox, Shannon Hall, Tom Lyons, Faron Hightower, Gary Bellenfant, Roy Carter, Phil Rapp, and all the others too numerous to mention.

To my husband, Tom and son, Zane for supporting me when my life as a cutting horse trainer wasn't always compatible with the roles of a traditional wife and mother. My most loving thank you.

Cutting One Run At A Time grew out of people's experiences — my own and many others. My sincerest thanks to all those who have gone before . . . from those who cut the first cattle out of the herd on the original ranches (and thought it was fun!) to the first pioneers of the National Cutting Horse Association.

TABLE OF CONTENTS

FOREWORD
by Paul Hansma

When it comes to cutting, being a good showman is ninety percent mental. It took me awhile to realize that. Being able to think under pressure and knowing how to prepare yourself is important if you want to be successful in the arena. Barbra Schulte learned that early on in her career.

I have known Barbra since 1985—back when I was working for Bill Riddle. I really got to know her when I started training cutting horses on my own in 1988. I would see her at a show, and she would help me study cattle. At this early time in my career, Barbra's way of speaking to me during my run was at just the right time. Her ability to assist me to locate specific cows gave me confidence in my own skills. The most important tool that Barbra gave me was the ability to focus on the job at hand—cutting the cows that we had selected—always in a positive, confidence-building manner. As a herd holder, she was an important member of my team.

Barbra told me about the Jim Loehr program and I listened. A lot of what he talks about is purely common sense. The little things sometimes get overlooked in high-pressure situations. But it is the little things that separate great showmen from the rest. I have listened to the programs Barbra has developed for cutters and I really believe in them. When you look at contestants in the finals of major events, they are not always riding the absolute best horses. Something in them comes out when they show. They look like winners, and they look like they belong in the finals.

I credit the Mentally Tough program with helping me to get where I am today. It keeps me calm and focused. For anyone out there just learning to cut, or for anyone wanting to learn how to be a better showman, I highly recommend this book. The basic fundamentals that Barbra is teaching are on the pages that follow. Barbra has a great way of identifying what works, what needs improvement, and, then arranging helpful information in small, easy-to-understand segments. She is a skilled communicator, and she doesn't make things too complicated. Making these basic skills habits, as I have, can have the same impact on your cutting.

Smithton, Illinois — 1962

The Hulling Family

Marie with Nicki, Cletus, Sr. with Cletus, Jr., Tootie with Bobbi, and Barbra

Sedalia, Missouri — 1969
Missouri State Fair
Barbra Hulling and Tammy Ann Cody

Photo courtesy of Roger Wilson

Springfield, Illinois — 1965
Illinois State Fair
Barbra Hulling and Jazzbo's Ruth

Photo courtesy of Ed Smyth

INTRODUCTION

I can say with absolute honesty that I have never experienced anything more exhilarating and fun than a great cutting run. I can also say that I have never experienced anything more frustrating than a horrible run. I remember well an incident when I was 14 years old. Despite lots of tuning, my cutting horse, Aledo Red Man, had a bad habit of coming way out at shows. At a weekend show in Benton, Illinois I walked back to the trailer alongside "Red Man" wailing, "Why did you run out to the turnback men . . . and then . . . ram my legs into the cattle when you fell back too far?!"

The joys and thrills of cutting far outweigh the bad times. My first exciting memory was showing a horse for Jim Lee in the Open Division of the Futurity when I was 18 years old. The mare was owned by a long-time family friend, Lem Anderson. I'll never forget the bright lights and applause at Will Rogers Coliseum in Fort Worth when I showed in the semi-finals. Obviously, Aledo Red Man's role in my life had been to toughen me up for the Futurity.

My career path with horses has been varied and wonderful. I have followed my many passions as I've woven them into a rather unique combination of riding, showing, teaching, writing, and exploring how to reach peak performance. The support of my family has allowed me to experiment with all of these things. Sometimes my explorations have been wise . . . other times not so hot. But through the unyielding assurance of my husband, Tom and son, Zane, I've been on an incredible journey in the horse world.

My career as a rider evolved from showing our family horses throughout college, to growing a 40-horse training operation as a professional, to riding a few select ones today. I'm not particularly gifted or athletic on a horse, so from childhood to the present moment, learning has been a challenge for me. Ironically, it has been those struggles to understand, and then practice, that have fueled my passion for teaching. Since I baptized myself as a professional cutting horse trainer in 1982, I have loved to teach.

What excites me most about teaching others is when someone comes to *know*—not try to convince themselves—that they really can do whatever it is they desire. I love seeing the lightbulb of understanding and knowing come on!

In early 1997, I embarked on a new journey, writing. I wanted to put on paper many of the ideas that worked for me and for others in my clinics. The product of these efforts (along with a lot of help from many people) is this book.

It is important for you understand that I offer the contents of this book as suggestions with the greatest humility. One of my highest personal values has been to withhold judgement of myself or others as being right or wrong. In the past, there have been strong cutting "camps" of thought about training, riding, and showing. I have never been a member of any camp. In fact, I have enjoyed observing and choosing what works for me. So, I present these ideas for your experimentation. Obviously, I believe in them. Take what works for you and don't worry about the rest. Relax.

I invited the champions and reserve champions of the open and non-pro divisions of weekend shows, limited aged events and the area workoffs to contribute to this book. I asked for their perspectives on all ten chapters. I am very appreciative of those who responded. For your enjoyment, their quotes are sprinkled throughout. I also included a few of my favorite quotes from people whose names you may or may not recognize.

My wish for you in your cutting life is that you always seek understanding and harmony within yourself and with your horse. You can never replicate an action consistently until you understand the "why" of what you're trying to do out there! Once you understand, the intent and approach must be to develop confidence and calmness—instead of fear and quick fixes. If you don't, you will never be consistently successful over time.

So, understand, really understand . . . then calm yourself, focus and try, try again. Enjoy the journey. There is no real destination where you finally arrive and have nowhere else to go. Have fun and learn each time you cut. Enjoy your horse beyond the show arena and all of the wonderful people in our sport.

I hope this book aids your journey.

This chapter helps you design your cutting experience.

It also discusses some common problems many cutters

experience and offers practical solutions.

"Keep cutting fun! The top athletes
in every sport love their sport and
enjoy practicing and competing."

Dick Gaines

CHAPTER 1 _____

DREAMS AND GOALS:
THE PROCESS OF BECOMING

We live in a world that focuses only on the bottom line. No
matter if we compete in the sports arena or the business arena,
most of us determine our success by measuring outward results.
Our sports heroes are those who win big or who have lucrative
product endorsements. In business, success is measured by the
money we make.

Goal setting for bottom-line results is an essential part of
achievement. However, it is only the beginning of an entire process which produces growth and success. One large, visible accomplishment is actually the compilation of many smaller achievements.

"I cut because there is nothing I would rather do. I hope to continue riding and training my own horses for as long as I enjoy it."

Sandy Bonelli

In cutting, I cannot produce a score of 76 on a particular run by concentrating on the score I want. To mark a 76, I must have my horse and myself ready, and then execute each part of my run, moment by moment, with excellence for two and one-half minutes.

Likewise, long-term improvement is the product of a long string of cutting achievements and lessons learned, one run at a time. Mastering the art of cutting is about putting together the many pieces of the cutting puzzle. Learning to cut is an evolving process. As you master the bits and pieces, along the way you learn what it takes to get the most out of cutting. And, as you'll learn in Chapter 5, having fun is the key ingredient in the process of being successful. Without a sense of enjoyment and fun, you get burned out and performance levels plummet.

Emotionally, it's easy to feel at the mercy of our most recent run. Cutting can seem like a huge lump that is either all good or all bad. We're either walking in the clouds or down in the dumps. But, a slight shift in thinking can balance the extreme highs and lows and can bring more success.

I suggest you focus on small, sequential steps that are within your control. Realize that no matter how hard you try, you don't have <u>direct</u> control over a goal like winning your event for the year-end or winning the Futurity. But you do have control over practicing critical skills like becoming more knowledgeable about cattle, making solid decisions during cuts, or sitting deeply and quietly on your horse—a few of the things that form the foundation

"Keep your goals realistic
and in perspective.
Use your goals as
building blocks to
progress yourself in the
cutting pen."

Corky Sokol

of winning runs.

You will learn more, win more, and enjoy the journey more as you begin to love the challenge of mastering the individual parts of cutting. As you let go and allow the pieces to come together when you show, you will encounter the magic of winning runs.

Different Strokes for Different Folks

I believe it's important to reflect on and honestly answer the following questions: What does cutting mean to me? Why do I cut? What do I want to accomplish?

As you reflect on those questions consider this. It's not about what cutting means to other people; it's about what cutting means to *you*. Your cutting goals should feel good to you. They may or may not be compatible with those around you. There will never be another person who will experience cutting in quite the same way as you. Each person's goals are uniquely their own.

Because people are different, individual goals fall into different categories based on personal preferences and competition levels. For the cutter who doesn't care to show but who instead prefers to "play" in his own arena, his goal may be to have fun with a group of cutting buddies on Saturday afternoon. For the 2,000 limit rider who enjoys local jackpots, his goal may be to some day show in — and win — a non-pro class. Others may wish to own a beautiful cutting ranch and have a world-class stallion to go with it. There are those who are committed to showing young horses. Anything

"I know God will not give me anything I can't handle. I just wish that he didn't trust me so much."

Mother Teresa

less than a top finish at the Futurity each and every year just won't do. <u>Of all these cutting goals, none is more valid or more important than another.</u> What is important is that the goals and dreams you set for yourself make *you* happy. Design your cutting program to support your goals. Satisfy your own personality and motivation level.

Take the time to think through the kind of cutting experiences you desire. That blueprint will provide you with personal guidelines to help you make the decisions necessary to arrive at your dreams. Without a clear picture of where you want to go with your cutting, it's easy to end up with a hodgepodge of experiences that are like leftover pieces to an unfinished puzzle. Set personally exciting goals and let them guide your decisions. Then get back to taking the smaller steps you have direct control over that add up to the big goals.

A Personal Leap of Faith

From 1982 through 1994, I was training and showing many young horses. I enjoyed what I did. But there was a part of my career that limited me. I found myself wanting to pursue some of my other loves.

In 1994, I shifted my career from training and showing lots of young horses to training and showing only a few. I decided to explore teaching the skills I learned in some Mentally Tough training I had done on my own. Because I saw how valuable the

"Set goals that you know you can accomplish and then be flexible and go even further."

Spencer Harden

training was, I wanted to teach these skills to riders in all disciplines. I also thought it would be fun to experience other parts of the vast and varied horse industry.

It was a scary, gut-wrenching decision to alter my career path. But the program was something I believed in, and it was part of what I really loved doing. I knew that developing this new portion of my career would take several years, so I took only a few outside horses for training.

It was difficult in many ways to alter what I had grown accustomed to doing as a professional trainer. Even though my heart was telling me that a new endeavor was what I wanted to do, I had to keep checking within *myself*. I had to have the ability to visualize my goal, the faith to create it, the commitment to make choices (both easy and hard) to support my goals at that moment, and the ability to say "no" to those things that did not take me towards my intended and desired direction. Shaping my career and life will always be an ongoing process, just as it is for you. I believe the key to joy and personal fulfillment is to make sure you keep checking in with yourself.

Today, I have different experiences and goals than I did during my first 12 years as a professional trainer. I enjoy training a few young horses owned by people whose goals are compatible with mine. I also show at major NCHA events and coach cutters at clinics. My work as a teacher, writer, and lecturer in the Mentally Tough program is fun for me. On occasion, I ride a dressage,

"Cutting is a lifestyle, not a business for me. I train cutting horses so that I may enjoy a quality lifestyle."

Gene Suiter

jumping, reining, or barrel horse.

The result is that I have more joy and more passion than ever before in my horse-career life. It's also made me fully aware of my passion for cutting and appreciative of how much I truly love the sport. Today, I'm doing most of the same things in cutting I've always done, but my career has taken on a much more personally defined twist. I'm closer to my family than ever before, and I enjoy a wide variety of personal and business activities.

I share this story with you because I see a lot of frustrated cutters at all levels of competition. One reason is the very nature of our sport. After you make a good run, it's easy to feel like you are on the highest of highs. But when you have one of those disastrous lost-a-cow-with-only-seconds-left or horse-quit-working runs, it is easy to feel as if you are sinking straight into the depths of the earth.

I also see people who are so frustrated with their cutting that they are thinking about hanging up their spurs. Most of the time that frustration is the product of a foggy personal vision or fuzzy goals. Those cutters spend unnecessary money on the wrong horse or funnel huge amounts of money into a training program that doesn't suit their needs.

Develop a clear idea about what you intend to experience in cutting. Be creative and seek out things that nourish your goals. Then you can avoid many of the pitfalls that could derail your cutting or knock your adventure off track. Once you have deter-

"The only death you die
is the death you die
everyday by not living.
Dream big and
dare to fail."

Norman Vaughan

mined where it is you want to be, situations and circumstances necessary to support those visions will present themselves. The choices you make for your cutting adventure have to come from within you and cannot be the product of someone else's hopes, desires, or plans.

Identify Your Cutting Goals

There are actions you can take that will help you arrive at your goals. These actions are your responsibilities. They are not the responsibilities of your trainer, your spouse, or your friends. To get the most out of cutting, here are three suggestions:

1. Identify where you want to start and where you want to go. Then talk to a variety of people to get different perspectives on how to get there.

2. Be creative and locate a number of opportunities to educate yourself about cutting. For example:

    ❑ Seek a mentor(s) to act as your guide. Search for and introduce yourself to successful individuals. Find out who trains in your area. Do your homework. Learn their individual niches, strengths, and weaknesses.

    ❑ Pore through cutting books and videos. Review them often. You will always find something new.

    ❑ Find out who offers clinics and when. Plan to participate in, or at least observe, as many clinics as possible to gain new perspectives. Attend educational

"I want my cutting experience to be fulfilling, if not, I quit. It will be time to move on if I can't get a high off the horses, the people and the atmosphere."

Lee Garner

lectures on different subjects in the equine industry.

❑ Read and understand the NCHA rule book and case book. Study it from cover to cover. The NCHA has also produced a judging videotape with examples of all rules.

3. Set long-term, measurable goals and short-term goals you can control. For example:

❑ Set long-term goals, but leave the dynamics open for change within your long-term plan. As you become more experienced, you may want to choose new directions.

❑ Identify what you need, what your horse needs, and how you are going to achieve those things.

❑ Focus on your weakest areas one practice session at a time and one run at a time.

Common Mistakes Cutters Make and Practical Solutions

Now that you're in touch with what you wish to create in your cutting life, here are some errors to avoid that many cutters make. I offer concrete solutions so that perhaps you can avoid these problems while you're on your way to achieving your dreams.

Mistake: *My green horse and I will learn together.*

One mistake that some new cutters make is that they want their horse and themselves to learn together. For example, a person may have a limited amount of money to purchase a horse. Instead of

"Cutting is the ultimate challenge on horseback. I want to respect myself for my efforts as well as gain respect from my peers. I desire to make a positive impact on all aspects of the cutting horse industry."

Winston Hansma

buying an older, more experienced, less expensive horse, the person goes for a colt. This plan usually doesn't work and leaves the cutter feeling insecure and incompetent in both his and his horse's ability. This is a situation that is almost always a set up for failure.

Solution: *Do your homework. Be patient.*

If you have come down with a severe case of "cutting fever" but you don't have a lot of money to spend on a horse, I suggest you don't rush out and buy the first inexpensive horse you ride, especially if it is an unfinished two- or three-year-old. Instead, start saving your money. Shop around. Ride different types of beginner horses. While your piggy bank grows fatter, contact a trainer in your area willing to give you lessons on a school horse in his barn.

There are three benefits to this approach. One, you satisfy that gnawing desire to cut. Two, you gain invaluable experience that will make you a better rider. And three, you will save money to put towards the right horse for you. In the interim, read, watch, and study everything you can about cutting. Beg, borrow, barter, do whatever it takes to satisfy the urge to cut, but don't rush out and buy the first green horse that comes along.

Mistake: *Enough money and a great horse will make me a winner.*

Another common mistake cutters make is assuming that deep financial pockets will assure success in the arena. While there is no doubt that owning a talented, well-trained, high-quality cutting

"When I first started to cut and compete, I always set attainable goals for myself. As time went on, my goals became more challenging. Cutting appeals to me because it tests me mentally and physically. Each run is always different and you never stop learning."

Carole Thorsnes

horse will stack the deck in your favor, it does not guarantee
success. With the beauty of owning a high-caliber horse comes the
same challenges that all cutters must face in competition — you
still must make split-second decisions that are grounded in experience. No amount of money can buy the experience it takes to put
together a winning run.

Solution: *Focus on building your skills.*

Understand that a horse is only part of the successful cutting
equation. Relax about winning only for the sake of winning.
Become focused on experiencing the process of cutting and learning all the aspects of this challenging sport instead of thinking you
can vault to the top of the ladder by merely buying a great horse.
Some of the greatest learning experiences happen during that slow,
methodical climb upward.

Having the power to buy a high-quality horse certainly can be a
wonderful asset to your program. But it is time, experience,
learning how to be comfortable in the herd, and riding your horse
well that will make you a threat to your competition. Love that
wonderful horse, but be patient with yourself, stay hungry for
knowledge, and experience will take care of the rest.

Mistake: *Living in the success/failure syndrome.*

Another common mistake cutters make is to allow themselves
to become discouraged to the point of wanting to quit when they
make not-so-good show runs over and over. I believe most people
have a problem identifying the *real* problems. They are unable to

"Results! Why, man, I have gotten a lot of results. I know several thousand that won't work."

Thomas Edison

separately evaluate the component parts of a cutting run. Instead
of seeing a run as pieces that make up a puzzle, they see the run as
a whole. Even though there may have been parts of the run that
were successful (good herdwork, riding with finesse out of a sticky
situation, clean quits), because the overall score was low, they
view the whole run as a failure. When cutters in this mindset have
a winning run, they are excited because they see the run as a
"success." But, ask the cutter to get back on the horse and repeat
the performance, and it is likely he can't. The same goes for poor
runs. The cutter can't identify parts of the run in need of improvement because he cannot dissect the run into its component parts.

Solution: ***Break it down.***

Approach a cutting run as if you are completing a puzzle.
When working a puzzle, you have a huge pile of pieces that,
somehow, fit together with time, patience, and dedication. You
continue to put pieces together until you find a combination that
fits. If you're missing a piece or pieces, the puzzle will have a
hole in it.

In cutting, focus on the elements and parts that make up a
competitive run rather than labeling a run as "success" or "failure"
based on your score. Identify what went well first. Then, identify
what you will do differently next time and how. By drawing your
focus to the individual parts of a run instead of trying to look at the
run as a whole, you will be able to quickly spot weaknesses and
then work to improve them.

"The greatest obstacle to
discovery is not ignorance -
it is the illusion of
knowledge."

Daniel J. Boorstin

Let's say a cutter is at a show and fails to properly warm up his horse. As a result of being too fresh or too tired, the horse has several misses during the run. Instead of recognizing that his poor score was caused in part by the fact that he did not properly prepare for the run before he entered the arena, the cutter gets mad at his horse, gets mad at the judge, and/or gets mad at his help. The cutter thinks he is a failure and wonders why he's even at the cutting. A better way to view this situation is to take responsibility and say to yourself, "OK, I had a miss out there, but it happened because I didn't warm up my horse well. But, I did feel good about my herdwork, and I knew what I needed to do in those bad cattle. Next time I will prepare my horse better."

Retrain yourself to focus on the elements and parts of a show run rather than trying to label it as a success or a failure based on the score. When you focus on the different aspects of a run, you quickly identify the strong parts as well as the weak links. Feel confident about the good stuff and then work to improve those weak parts.

Mistake: *The judge is a jerk.*

Sometimes when cutters make poor runs they refuse to take responsibility for the negative aspects of the run. Instead, they blame something or someone else. They might blame their horse, their trainer, their spouse, their help, the judge, or the ground for their poor performance.

"I enjoy breeding winning horses with ability and brains. A bonus is riding them and winning!"

Helen Groves

Solution: *Take responsibility.*

In the world of sport science, the process of blaming others repeatedly has the most sabotaging effects on your ability to perform. The key is to look objectively at what occurred. Decide what was under your control and what was not. For example, you cannot control other people including trainers, helpers and judges, nor can you control ground conditions. The only thing you have control over is how you respond to your horse, your trainer, your spouse, the judge or the ground conditions. The more positive you stay, the more positive and consistent your results will be.

Quit blaming others for events and situations. Instead, take sole responsibility for how you process what happens in your world. Become skilled at turning negatives into positives and enjoy cutting.

Mistake: *I'm in the big bucks now.*

Many new hopefuls may view cutting as a money-making proposition. They put unnecessary pressure on themselves or on trainers because they believe they must stay in the black. While there are those who do make their living riding, selling, and show-ing cutting horses, if you wish to enter this business and be listed in *Fortune 500* next year, you may be in for quite a surprise.

Solution: *Do your homework.*

Research expenses and probable income. Know that you can count on projected expenses and then some, and you can't always count on projected income. Then make your decision about

"I cut for the <u>thrill</u> of cutting."

Kobie Wood

jumping into cutting as a <u>business</u>. I suggest you decide to live peacefully, knowing that the money you put into your horses will probably not be a money-making venture. You may even want to overestimate expenses and underestimate income. In the beginning, view cutting as a hobby. Do your homework and make financial decisions that are wise, so you don't waste your money. If, with time and experience, you wish to make cutting a business, go for it. But, make this a business only after you have had some time to experience the ups and downs of our sport firsthand.

<u>Mistake</u>:   *The world is coming to an end. I just marked a 60.*

Do you believe that your life's happiness is determined by your success in the cutting arena? While this may sound like an extreme statement, some tend to feel only as good as their last run.

<u>Solution:</u>   *Lighten up.*

Your value as a human is not determined by any cutting run you will ever make. Period. The essence of life is not decided by your most recent successful or unsuccessful competition. People cut because it is a personal challenge, or they love horses, or they strive for excellence in the arena. But, cutting is never more than that. Your spirituality, your family, your health, and your friends are the core of life. The way in which you value those things is the value of life. Cutting allows you to challenge yourself, love horses, share friendships, and have fun.

When the inevitable bomb crashes in the cutting arena, keep

"I cut for the excitement of cutting and to be with friends that I have made through the years."

Bobby Hawkins

this in mind: no matter how bad it was, there will be a tomorrow and there will be another cutting. Set a time limit in which anger or frustration within yourself is allowed. After that time is up, "get over it" and move on. By letting go of anger and frustration you will come to realize that no matter who you are, there will be many lost cattle in your career. Even people who aren't baseball fans know that Babe Ruth once held two baseball records. Not only did he hit the most home runs, but he also had the most strike-outs.

Have Fun and Be Yourself

In setting goals, create a cutting program that works best for you. Be creative and seek ways to reach your goals, efficiently and effectively. Be patient with your horse and yourself as you learn and grow as a cutter. Enjoy the process and surround yourself with people who make you happy. Have fun! Keep checking in with yourself to see that you stay on the right path as your dreams grow and change.

Now that you have grounded yourself in your dreams, it's time to expand your horizons to include a wonderful support system that will be instrumental in taking you where you'd like to go.

This chapter discusses the powerful, positive effects

of developing a strong support system.

"To build a successful program, you need the unselfish support and input from everyone involved — your horseshoer, veterinarian, all your help back at the barn, your turnback help and herdholders, and last but not least, the owners of your horses. Without everyone's 100% commitment, success will be hard to achieve."

Winston Hansma

CHAPTER 2

BUILD A STRONG SUPPORT SYSTEM

In cutting, we depend on those who surround us. Cutting is the only equestrian sport where the rider has four helpers in the show arena. Beyond our helpers, every one of us has a support system that consists of mentors, family, and friends. We spend a great deal of time pursuing our challenges with these people.

The people who make up our families are, for the most part, predetermined (of course). But, the other people surrounding us— our mentors, our friends, and our helpers in the show arena—are chosen. The choices we make are key. They shade and color how our cutting experiences unfold. Although you can never control

Confidence-Building Wisdom

◆   Our greatest opportunities to learn are hidden in difficulties and disappointments;

◆ Our lives are enhanced by those who are fun to be with and who provide moral support;

◆ Confidence grows among friends. It vanishes in the presence of those who criticize us;

◆ Confidence grows where there is safety and acceptance;

◆ Confidence is built by supporting strengths and offering positive suggestions for areas of improvement. Focusing on weaknesses diminishes confidence;

◆ When we praise and give positive "to do" suggestions for incorrect actions, we open doors to greater achievement;

◆ When we negatively criticize one another, doors to greater achievement are slammed shut.

other people, there are two things you can control: with whom you choose to spend time, and how you process what is said by those who surround you.

Confidence and fun are two positive emotions that ignite cutting success. The people you choose to cut with are instrumental in building and maintaining your confidence and cultivating a sense of fun and enjoyment. From friends to trainers, other people make a huge contribution to your mental and emotional cutting environment. Life is about giving, learning, constantly improving, and having fun. It's about sharing yourself and your time to help other people.

Mentors

Even if you do not have a trainer, you need a mentor. A mentor is a person you respect and from whom you seek advice. Even the highest-level trainers have a circle of people who provide feedback. As you process information from others, you develop your uniqueness. Therefore, it is important that the information you seek comes from those whose opinions you respect.

I suggest that you choose an eclectic group of people. Each will give you information from a different perspective. Then, it is your responsibility to wade through the information you receive, take what works for you, and discard the rest to develop your style. Because so many people volunteer their opinions, I cannot over-emphasize how important it is to sort through the information and

"Success occurs in clusters and is born in generosity."

Julia Cameron

feedback you receive; then select the parts that complement your personal values and conform with your style of cutting. Don't get caught up in the right or the wrong of the information. Simply search for people and ideas that promote harmony with your horse and confidence within yourself.

Trainers/Instructors

The discussion here will focus on meeting your needs as a student. It is not a discussion about choosing a trainer based on his or her horse training skill. Although I'll focus on your learning needs in this chapter, I recommend that every consideration be taken to find a trainer who builds your horse's style and confidence, too. Do your homework and search for a trainer who is great with both you and your horse.

Good instructors truly care about your cutting progress and how well or how poorly you perform. They believe in you. They believe you can reach your goals. They are the ones who understand the principles of cutting as a sport, both training and showing. They know how to apply those principles for cutters at any skill level. They encourage you to rise to even their level of expertise. Your success offers them no threat.

Great instructors have the ability to communicate. When they give a lesson, they can articulate the focus of the lesson and can demonstrate it, if necessary. They encourage you to ask "Why?" and they will gladly explain the answer. They are quick to point

"Find a
trainer that
you feel
comfortable
with."

Corky Sokol

out positive aspects of your riding, both before and after your ride. When they coach, they are clear about what they want you to do. They do not dwell on negatives, but instead focus on the positive by explaining or showing the correct maneuver. Instructors show and coach you on the how and the why so that you understand not only how, for example, using your hands, your seat position, or your leg position will affect your horse, but also why. With that knowledge, you can practice and repeat the maneuver with confidence because you understand.

Instructor Selection Tips

We spend a lot of time working with a trainer to improve our technical skills. Ideally, choose a trainer who knows how to keep things fun while offering moral support. I'm not talking about baby-sitting. I'm talking about choosing someone who believes in you, who cares, and who knows his or her stuff about training and showing, but who also understands the power of positive emotions in learning and showing. It's not a right or wrong issue. It's a "what fits me" issue.

Consider the following when selecting an instructor:

1. *Reflect on your personal values.*

Is an instructor's attitude or teaching style important to you? Do you want to be involved in the physical care of your horse? For example, some trainers are very strict in their approach to veterinary medicine. Others combine a traditional approach with

Understand the "Why"

No student can effectively repeat an action with confidence unless they understand the "why" of that lesson.

alternative treatments such as chiropractic care, acupuncture, or the use of other types of alternative therapies and medicine. What's important to you?

Are the training methods confidence-building for your horse? What is your expectation for communication from a trainer? Some trainers may keep your horse and call only if there is a medical emergency. Is it important that they call you to let you know how your horse is working or are you going to do the calling? Whatever the criteria, you must be clear about what is important to you. List your values and then prioritize them. Work with a trainer who fulfills the most important ones. Chances are, like getting married, there's no perfect match. But don't compromise on your most important values.

2. Are your schedules compatible?

Do you and the trainer go to the same shows? Some specialize in weekend cuttings and have a predictable show schedule. Some trainers show only in aged events. Others go to weekend shows in addition to aged events. Do you want to work with a trainer who will be at the shows you attend and who can help you there? Or, do you only plan to get lessons from that person and rely on your own skills at a show? You must decide what works best for you.

It is also important for you to know how a trainer's barn works as far as saddling and loping. Some trainers provide full service while others expect you to saddle and warm-up your own horse prior to a lesson or before showing. If you are making the same

"You need to have people around that will surround you in a positive atmosphere."

Paul Hansma

show circuit, are you expected to haul your own horse? If you live close to the trainer, find out if he or she would like you to help turn-back or herd-hold. Some trainers think that is great; others don't.

3. *What teaching style do you prefer?*

Some trainers are very authoritative in their instructional style—it's their way or the highway. Other trainers are very interactive in their approach—they enjoy talking it over. Still others are very reserved, easy-going, and quiet. Often the latter does not have a clear teaching style, and you are left to glean information based entirely on what you observe. What style suits you best?

4. *Research your trainer's background.*

Talk directly with a trainer to understand their career experience. Interview a number of people—both clients and non-clients—and ask questions based on things that are important to you. When you interview more than one person you will get a broad idea of someone instead of skewed, slanted information. Watch the trainer as they work horses and as they work with others to see what kind of instructor he or she is and what kind of training style the person has. If you should come up with two trainers who measure up equally, rely on your instincts to make the decision.

5. *Always be honest and upfront.*

You have a responsibility to maintain a professional relationship with a trainer. Most trainers are fully aware that every person

"The most critical attribute any member of your support team must possess is honesty. You need someone who tells you the truth - if you made a bad cut, you're leaning, or your run's picture is negative because your horse is rolling, not stopping, etc. You don't need a trainer or your help to say, 'You're looking great. That judge doesn't know what he or she is doing!' or 'The cattle are too bad to mark anything on.' You have to know the truth so you can improve, and that's the name of the game when you are learning any skill."

Lindy Burch

and every horse will not be compatible with their training program. From a trainer's perspective, it is difficult when the news of a client's impending change (large or small) comes from other people. No matter how difficult it may be, communicate and be honest. If a trainer and a particular horse don't work well together, discuss it first with the trainer. Perhaps a different program would work better for a particular horse. Communication is key.

Your Support System

No matter how wonderful your relationship is with your trainer or anyone else in your support system, problems do arise. It's up to you to nip them in the bud. Communication between trainers and clients or between riders and their family members or friends can become strained at times. If negative feelings are not eliminated, the strain can turn into ill will. If strong, negative emotions are rampant when positive emotions are critical to your showing, your performance will go downhill.

Many people in our lives have good intentions but are uninformed about how important positive emotions are to success. While you can never control other people, use the following strategies to promote positive emotions and good communication between yourself and those closest to your cutting life when problems come up . . . and they always will!

"No one can get very far without support from others and cutting is no different. Treat everyone with respect and fairness and you will be able to get help and support anywhere and anytime you need it."

Dick Gaines

Ways to Promote Good Communication
When Problems Arise

1. *Schedule a meeting with the family member, trainer, or friend you are having a problem with.*

Decide what time would be best for a meeting. Select a time when emotions are even and pressure is lowest. Avoid confrontations during the heat of the moment, i.e., during a show, because negative emotions run highest then. After making a bad run, take a deep breath and let the moment pass. Find solutions during more neutral times.

2. *Know what you want.*

Be clear about what you would like to gain before you ever start your meeting. For example, are you concerned about your horse's training or how you want to be coached or both? Whatever the situation, determine your goal. Clarity and simplicity will keep things uncluttered. If there are a number of concerns, choose only one or two of the most difficult and save the others for a later time.

3. *Explain your situation.*

Begin by stating that the goal of the meeting is to promote understanding and ease for both of you. State your case with the intention to find common ground for solutions. First, ask how they see you in your situation. Be ready to listen. Remind yourself to be open to suggestions and be sure and listen to the other person's point of view. This will open up communication. Draw the other person out by first asking questions to determine their perspective on the situation.

"You have to have a strong support group. You have to be able to express your feelings - good and bad - to your trainer and all of your help."

Bobby Hawkins

4. *Exchange possible solutions.*

After you have listened to the other person's view, suggest solutions based on meeting both of your most important needs. Listen to their solutions. Give the person you are communicating with room for negotiation.

5. *Add support.*

Remind him or her how much you support them. Ask if there are other things you could do to better show that support. Being nonjudgmental and encouraging will open communication pathways.

6. *Kiss— (Keep it short and simple, that is).*

Exchange information. Make your points. Find solutions. Exit on a good note. If you don't reach the outcome you had hoped for, at least you gave it your best effort and left the door open.

7. *Take responsibility for your own positive environment.*

This may be the most important point of all! Cutters who don't state their needs and then take responsibility for meeting those needs rarely reap benefits from their support system. Don't blame others for your situation.

Easy, positive relationships between people in our cutting lives can provide immeasurable joy and much-needed encouragement.

"In helping others, we shall help ourselves, for whatever good we give out completes the circle and comes back to us."

Flora Edwards

<u>Nine Tips for Becoming a Better Student</u>

Now that we've discussed trainers' and mentors' roles, here are some practical suggestions you can do to fulfill your end of the deal as a student of cutting.

1. *Set long-term riding goals that really excite you.*

Create a picture in your mind of the kind of rider you want to be and the kind of cutting experiences you want to have. When you start feeling droopy about your cutting, call up these images of yourself riding like a champion and get the positive, emotional fires burning again. This step is as important as anything else you will ever do in your cutting because whether you consciously plan it or not, you become what you think. Take charge, create dynamic self images, and keep them in the front of your mind.

2. *Set short-term (daily, monthly, per lesson) goals.*

Focus on results over which you have control such as staying relaxed, or executing a specific technique. These are called performance goals. Talk to your trainer or mentor and prioritize the order of your work by addressing your weakest areas first.

3. *Always focus on the behavior or skill you want to learn . . . do not dwell on what you don't want to happen.*

Most people worry about what they fear and create that situation in their mind, over and over again. Visualize and/or talk to yourself about what you desire to achieve. This approach is one of the most powerful learning tools you can put to work for yourself. The first step is to recognize when you are dwelling on negative

"Because I don't have an overabundance of confidence, I need people around me who are positive thinkers and support me even when I'm not winning. I like to come home after a successful or not-so-successful trip and know that my family and friends don't place much importance on the end result. Real life awaits me at home, so I put cutting results away and focus on training my colts and my tennis game."

Sandy Bonelli

thoughts. The second step is to replace those thoughts with words and visions of the appropriate, positive action.

4. *Evaluate your riding progress after each riding session.*

Make sure you recognize progress. Feel good about that! Identify what is good but needs more practice. What isn't working? These answers indicate areas to work on next time. Choose only one or two of the weakest areas. This approach keeps you focused on things you can control and keeps your progress consistent. And, by the way, this process never ends. So, loosen up! Don't fear your mistakes and keep improving.

5. *Make sure you completely relax between cattle.*

Train yourself (and your horse) at home to have an automatic, brief relaxation time between cuts. Simply stop, breathe, and consciously relax. Research shows that training recovery is as important as training specific skills. When you train instant relaxation between cattle at home, it carries over to the show arena.

6. *Always take your time.*

Your mind and body will stay relaxed, allowing your learning to be most effective. Hurried practice sessions may or may not really help you.

7. *When you feel tired, practice for short intervals or do not practice at all.*

Fatigue produces a number of negative emotional states which reduce your ability to learn. Often, an inability to stay focused and

"My dad has had the greatest influence on me, as well as giving me sound advice. He always said you can learn something from everybody, it's just a process of keeping the good and throwing out the bad. The relationships you make with people in cutting last a lifetime."

Dick Cogdell

perform well can be traced to fatigue.

8. *Stay positive by knowing that your errors are only indicators of where to focus your improvements next time.*

See them as opportunities to excel as you meet your current challenges. You could even be so bold as to welcome the tough times! This change in perception and attitude could bolster your performance immensely because you have replaced fear with challenge.

9. *Most importantly, HAVE FUN.*

In fact, have a blast! Nothing— absolutely nothing—is more critical to learning to cut than maintaining a sense of joy and humor in your riding.

11 Practical Tips for Family Members, Trainers, and Friends to Encourage a Cutter

Whether you are a trainer or a spouse, friend, or parent of a cutter, here are some easy ways to help build up a cutter's confidence.

1. *Get in touch with what motivates someone.*

What excites them? Why do they cut? What do they want to gain from their riding experience? Everyone is different. Connect personally to your rider's vision and desires first.

2. *Believe in the person you are coaching.*

Believe he or she can excel. Realize that your sincere belief

**"Support from
your family and
loved ones is
like no other
support you
can have."**

Millie Kay Bouget

and caring shows naturally in your attitude. Great coaches do all
they can to assist someone even if it means surpassing their own
levels of achievement.

3. *Prior to a lesson or show, discuss goals over which the
rider has control.*

At shows, focus on preparation and showing ideas for the horse
and the rider; i.e., staying calm on the cut with eyes focused on the
cattle in the center of the arena, not on things like bad weather, the
judge, or other people.

4. *Build skills sequentially.*

Set goals according to what is most important for the rider to
achieve first in order to shore up his or her weakest areas. Then
proceed through successive, small steps.

5. *Give suggestions and instructions positively.*

Focus clearly on what you want the cutter to achieve, not on
what you don't want. For example, if you suggest to someone to
"stop leaning," you plant a picture in their mind of leaning. If you
suggest staying soft and centered deep in the saddle, you help him
or her feel balance and rhythm. When you coach consistently by
giving clear suggestions of "what to do" instead of "what not to
do," you become a powerful mentor. Listen to yourself to catch
negative phrases. If you hear yourself talking about what "not to
do," simply replace the negative with the desired positive action of
the moment.

"My family is glued at the hip. My entire family's success is based on honesty with each other."

Kathy Boone

6. *Provide confidence-building feedback after a session or event.*

First, comment positively on the good things that happened. Give the cutter a clear review of what was effective before you give suggestions for the less than desirable things that occurred. Be specific and matter-of-fact about what would be the best thing to do in a similar situation. Help cutters think in terms of specific replacements and not in generalities. Challenge them to view themselves as someone who will always have challenges to improve their riding—just like all accomplished cutters. The joy of cutting is found in a passion to improve as well as in winning an event.

7. *Assist the cutter in relaxing between cattle for a few moments.*

This is known as recovery and it is the time when a person collects himself and maximizes his ability to be focused on the next cut. Remind the cutter to train himself to relax between cattle.

8. *Maintain your poise and calmness in all situations.*

Your approach to any situation can powerfully influence a cutter's emotional environment. No matter how busy you are or how little time is available, act cool on the outside even if you're going a little crazy on the inside!

9. *Beware of energy levels and emotional states.*

Many trainers and helpers make the mistake of becoming so

"Cutting's greatest reward is the friendships one develops with fellow competitors."

Phil Feinberg

involved with the technical parts of riding that they tune out how a rider is feeling and their energy level. If energy levels are low or the emotional state is on the down side, address those issues first. High-energy, negative emotions like anger, defensiveness, and fear, as well as low-energy, negative emotions like feelings of blame or being burned out, greatly impact a rider's ability to deliver a peak performance.

10. *Develop an attitude of challenge for the tough times.*

Difficulties come in all shapes and sizes. Some are on-going while others seem to pop up out of nowhere. Whatever the problem, help the cutter view it as a challenge as well as an opportunity to excel and be creative. Great performers in all sports challenge the "gremlins of doom" when they appear. When everything is falling apart around the person you are helping, help him or her develop the motto "I love this! If I can handle this situation, I can handle anything." That is the way a champion thinks.

11. *Most importantly, have fun.*

Nothing is more critical to helping others than keeping things fun. Create a sense of joy, humor, and playfulness. It will keep your own attitude positive and it can be tremendously contagious to everyone around you.

In the next chapter, I will help you learn how to look for a horse that suits your situation and how to avoid making common purchase errors. After all, cutting is a lot more fun and productive when you are riding a horse that suits you.

This chapter is about learning how to look for a

horse that suits you and how to avoid making

common purchasing errors.

"The key to winning is a great horse that fits you and your
style of riding. I don't believe that all of us can train any
horse and the key is to find that horse that suits you.
Don't buy a horse just because someone else wins on it.
Make sure that horse will cut for you, too."

Sandy Bonelli

CHAPTER 3 _____

CHOOSE A HORSE THAT SUITS YOUR NEEDS

One of the most common errors people make in cutting is
attempting to develop skill and confidence with a horse that is not
suited for them. If you find yourself in this predicament, have
faith. There could be many reasons why you and your horse don't
"fit" each other. You may be riding a horse that is incompatible
with you because you or someone else made an honest error in
judgment at the time of purchase. Or, maybe the horse was bought
at a sale or show based strictly on impulse and emotion.

Cutting horses vary in so many ways. They range in age,
shape, and size. There are weanling prospects and 20-year-old

"Look for the same qualities in a good horse you would look for in a good friend. Honesty, consistency, effort, and heart."

Winston Hansma

veterans. Just like people, horses have different temperaments, different training backgrounds, and different showing histories. Some have had a lot of owners while others have had few. There is no universal horse. What matters is that the horse you choose supports and complements where you are in your learning and showing.

Some cutters are thrilled to own only one horse and that horse must meet all of his or her needs, from practice to show. Other cutters have the luxury of owning several horses; one to practice on and one or more for showing. There is no right or wrong scenario. You can learn to make wise purchasing decisions, design a program that optimizes your personal learning and showing goals, and meet your financial capabilities.

Why it is Important to Ride a Horse that Fits Your Needs

Riding the right horse builds your confidence, keeps cutting fun, and allows you to enjoy horses in general. If you choose a horse that is not well suited for you, your confidence could be greatly diminished. If things become uncomfortable, it might cause you to want to quit. Perhaps you have toyed with the idea of hanging up your chaps and spurs because you think you do not have the ability to cut. The reality may be that the horse you are riding does not fit your needs at this point in your career. If cutting is not as much fun as you would like for it to be, take an objective look at the horse you are riding.

"I've always had to put in lots of time and effort in becoming familiar with a horse; and maybe more importantly, having a horse become comfortable and familiar with my needs, balance, timing, level of aggression, etc. Comfort levels need to unite."

Mary Jo Milner

I'm not saying to blame the shortcomings of your cutting on your horse. You may have a perfectly wonderful horse that is just not the right horse for you. Or, perhaps the horse you ride has challenges that cannot be overcome by you or anyone else in your circle of resources. No one—not the horse, not the trainer, not you—has to be the bad guy. It just might be time to move forward and find a more suitable horse.

In order for your cutting to prosper, your horse must have the personality and experience to meet your cutting and showing needs while still presenting you with an element of challenge.

Primary Considerations for Your Horse Selection

1. *The horse has more experience than you* (unless you are training young horses).

Most people need a horse that has been seasoned enough to confidently handle the tough cattle and unusual situations that develop in competition.

2. *The horse has good, balanced conformation.*

Horses who have classic, positive conformation qualities are preferable because they usually hold up better to the physical stress of cutting. They are also more marketable for re-sale. Some of the most important conformation characteristics are strong bone structure, short cannon bones, a short back, a long hip, medium to long neck, straight legs, and good feet.

3. *The horse is sound* (or requires relatively low physical

"The horse is the most important factor involved in cutting. I see a lot of people buy a $150,000.00 truck and trailer, new saddles, chaps, etc. Yet they buy a $15,000.00 horse and then can't understand why they don't win. The judges don't check the parking lots."

Dick Gaines

maintenance).

Most cutting horses are less-than-perfect specimens physically. But some problems are more serious and require more upkeep than others. Trust the professional opinion of your veterinarian when selecting a horse. Never skip the vet check prior to exchanging a check for a horse.

4. *The horse suits your personality.*

Sometimes a high-strung person is better suited to a quieter horse while a calm person may be better able to get in sync with an energized horse. A very high-strung horse paired with a very high-strung rider often spells trouble.

5. *The horse excites you.*

You look forward to going to the barn because he's there—even when it's time to feed, groom, or clean stalls.

6. *The horse is easy to ride.*

A suitable horse is easy for you to ride on cattle but still challenges your ability.

7. *The horse is fun to ride both in and out of the arena.*

Although there is no feeling like a great run, much of the time you spend with your horse will not be on cattle. A horse who is easy to ride and who is easy to be around makes your entire cutting experience that much more pleasurable.

8. *The horse isn't show smart.*

You want to avoid purchasing a horse that decides to go on a mental vacation when you enter the show arena; i.e., coming out,

Dare To Make Mistakes

It is important to understand that the process of learning to cut naturally involves making errors such as spurring at the wrong time, gripping too much with your legs, losing your balance, or riding with one leg more than the other. In order to learn, you must feel free to make mistakes and then learn from them. It is also vital to understand and accept that those errors might (not always) decrease your horse's value when it comes time to re-sell because he picked up undesirable behaviors you unintentionally created. To maintain your horse's value, seek assistance from a professional trainer or mentor to help you keep your horse on track. Balance your practice time with the horse's professional tune-up time. But the sooner you stop worrying you will ruin the horse, the quicker you will progress. You may or may not negatively affect your horse and his resale value. Only time will tell. Let go of those concerns so you can learn. Buy a horse that you aren't afraid to make mistakes on, and "go for it."

making loopy turns, falling back into the herd, or shorting out on the ends. Most often those problems are the result of the horse being conditioned to do those things in the show arena by a rider who was inexperienced and inadvertently gave him the wrong signals, repeatedly.

9. *The horse is within your price range.*

Be careful here. Stay controlled. If you're financially strung out, it can quickly zap the fun out of showing.

Secondary Considerations for Your Horse Selection

There are other factors that should be considered when buying a horse, but they are not as critical as those above.

1. *Size*

If you have an extra-small or extra-large body type, size may be an important factor to consider in your choice of a horse. Otherwise, as a general rule, stay within the range of 14.1 to 15-hand horses.

2. *Gender*

Geldings, by nature, are more predictable day to day. They do not have the raging hormones to contend with that mares and studs sometimes do. A gelding's greatest attribute is his steadfastness, and it is a point to strongly consider.

Some people prefer mares because they have more innate market value than geldings due to their breeding potential. Some mares (not all) tend to be unpredictable and perform differently

Good Investments

1. Mares out of sires and dams who are proven winners and producers. Geldings with great bloodlines are good investments, too, but their value lies primarily in their performance ability.

2. Horses who have experienced a strong, consistent training program in their two- and three-year-old years. Early, solid fundamentals in a confidence-building program are the keys to a horse's longevity in the show arena.

3. Horses shown or seasoned as three-, four-, and five-year-olds in fresh cattle novice classes on weekends, or in aged events, while in a consistent training program.

4. Horses owned by only one or two different owners. Usually this suggests a great amount of stability and consistency in their training and showing.

when they are cycling. The strong point about owning a mare is that if she gets seriously injured, she can be bred. Just make sure that you would like to produce another horse like your mare!

Studs are their own breed of cat. Do your homework and proceed with caution.

3. *Habit Tolerance*

Some horses crib and may have to wear a cribbing strap. Others peck at the trailer. Some pull back and make tying them up a real problem. Others kick at other horses. Different people are more tolerant of unusual habits and quirks in horses. It is totally individual. Consider how serious the habit is, how much you like the horse, how patient you are, and then decide which habits you can tolerate and which ones you can't.

4. *Color*

If you love sorrels but hate bays, don't buy a bay unless you can't live without him. Although such a preference is very minor, it can make a big difference if color is important to you.

How to Choose the Right Horse

1. *Decide what kind of horse you "need" first and "want" second.*

I have a woman friend who showed me a list she had compiled of characteristics of the type of man she sought! It read: spiritual, great job, super sense of humor, good looking, independent, no children, etc. After about six months of searching, she found her

"A great cutting team - horse and rider - is more than the sum of each. The intangibles of trust and faith, one in the other, are equally important."

Dan Lufkin

mate and later got married. That may seem like an extreme idea, but the same principle can apply to seeking a particular type of horse. Take out a piece of paper and write down all the things you are looking for in a horse. Consider everything I have discussed so far. If you are not sure what you are looking for, ask several trusted professionals or people whose opinions you value.

I urge you to combine their ideas and suggestions with your own instincts. You may also write down things that you want in a horse as they come to mind such as sorrel, small, big hip, nice head, good bone structure, solid training foundation, etc. After you compile a list, go back and rank the things you wrote down so that you are clear on what is negotiable and what isn't. For example, a solid training foundation may be something you can't live without; you would like a mare but you would take a gelding if he was right; and, the sorrel color would be nice but it is totally flexible.

2. *Decide how you will conduct your search.*

You can do it on your own, or you can solicit the opinions of several successful and experienced friends, mentors, or trainers. If you conduct your search with a professional, choose someone you trust. Be sure to confirm your financial arrangement up front. Standard commission is ten percent usually (but not always) paid by the seller. When financial matters are settled up front, you avoid distrust, misunderstandings, and hard feelings.

You can also purchase a horse through an auction. Just make

"Do not lie to your horse and do not lie to yourself about your horse. If he or she is not the one for you, get another one."

Gene Suiter

sure you do your homework. Look at the consignment list in advance, research who is involved with the horse, and dig deep for information on training, showing, and soundness. You may request a video from the seller and/or you may be able to arrange to watch the horse work more than just on the day of the sale. Auctions provide an excellent marketplace for purchasing horses, but to minimize the possibility of making an emotional purchase that will result in problems, do your research prior to the sale. If your purchase is made solely on first impressions and emotions, you may or may not end up with the horse you think you are buying.

3.   *Be patient.*

Once you write a check for a horse, that horse is in your barn and becomes a part of your expense account. Take your time. Wait until you feel that a particular horse fits most of your desires. A good rule of thumb when shopping for a cutting horse is to put the horse's weakest attributes under a microscope prior to the purchase. No horse is perfect. Investigate and take a close look before you write the check.

Don't make poor choices in judgment because you are in a hurry. Again, cutting is so much more fun when you are riding a horse that suits you.

What To Do With a Horse That Doesn't Suit You

Sometimes, no matter how much research you put into buying a horse, you end up with one that just doesn't work for you. This

"Smart, especially cow smart qualities in a cutting horse, makes up for a multitude of other deficiencies."

Phil Feinberg

will probably be part of your cutting experience if you own a number of horses over time. The key is to learn from errors and move on. Don't get caught up in trying to make the horse something he is not.

Be realistic and consider the following:

1. *When things do not seem to be working out, make a decision to move on by giving "x" amount of time (i.e., three months) to the compatibility of the relationship.*

Seek professional help, attend a clinic or get advice from people you respect. If, over that predetermined amount of time, things work out, great. If not, move on to step two.

2. *Research the best way to sell the horse.*

   Options include:

   ❑ selling the horse privately through word-of-mouth or advertising

   ❑ selling the horse through a trainer

   ❑ selling the horse through an auction

3. *Sell your horse.*

Let go of any regret or insecurities on your part, i.e., "I should have been able to . . . ." It's only cutting. Learn. Accept things that happen. Move on and enjoy the next horse and the next experiences to come.

Now that you're equipped with a vision, a great support system and a horse for you, you're ready to develop superb basic riding skills.

This chapter is a discussion of basic horsemanship skills with specific emphasis on their use in cutting. It is divided into two sections. The first identifies correct body position (form) and the affects on the horse (function). The second section identifies basic warm-up maneuvers that allow you to communicate with your horse, both in and out of the cutting arena.

"The better rider you become, the less you will worry about riding while cutting. If you're worried about hanging on, you can't concentrate on the cattle or cutting."

Corky Sokol

CHAPTER 4 _____

DEVELOP BASIC RIDING SKILLS

There are several books on the market that cover horsemanship in great detail. The comments I make in this chapter only skim the surface. But, I do want to emphasize some basic skills that I feel are important. While these skills may seem less exciting than cutting, they form the very foundation (or lack thereof) of your success in the show arena. The potential performance of you and your horse will be at its highest only when your basic riding skills come instinctively.

I'll begin by identifying how to find and maintain your center of balance. Then, I will discuss how the rest of your body comple-

"When riding a horse, one of the most important things to learn is balance. Without balance, you will not be able to show your horse with any skill."

Paul Hansma

ments your center of balance. You will be introduced to and begin to understand some additional basic riding skills, how to execute them, and what effect they have on your horse. It is critical that you practice these skills diligently—they are the core of your cutting. You become consistent in the show pen when you get in tune with your horse outside the show pen.

For example, when your center of balance is properly anchored, your legs will be in the correct position and your upper body will be aligned. Those positions *allow* your horse to do his job. When your center of balance is off, your upper body is naturally out of alignment, your legs and arms are stiff, and you inhibit your horse. Sometimes the effects are minor and your horse is only slightly off. But, at other times, rider errors can give a horse confusing or incorrect messages. As a result, your horse might miss, come out, or run off.

Often, our horses are unfairly blamed for our errors. I urge you to be fair to yourself and your horse and master the basic riding skills outlined in this chapter. As you develop synchronism with your horse outside the arena, watch the results carry over naturally into practice and show situations.

As you read this chapter, follow these steps in your learning:

1. Intellectually understand correct riding positions while in the saddle.

2. Know and be able to physically find the correct position on demand.

A major influence on my riding and

teaching came from Sally Swift's

book, Centered Riding. Now in her

80's, Sally has studied and taught

riding her entire life. Although her

riding discipline is dressage, her teach-

ings are universal in terms of form

and function for riding. She uses nu-

merous mental imagery examples

which illicit feel within the rider. For

a more detailed study on basic riding

skills, I highly recommend this book.

3. As you ride, consistently monitor yourself, remaining cognizant of when you are correct or incorrect.

4. If you check in with yourself and know you are correct, continue on and experience the feeling. If you check in with yourself and you know you are incorrect—no problem! Just make the necessary adjustments. Be kind to yourself as you learn. Keep self-monitoring and self-correcting as long as it takes to master the skills.

5. Let go. Allow yourself to feel your horse and find synchrony and rhythm in your riding.

During these next two sections, I will be very systematic in my approach to describing form, function, and feel. I will tell you *what,* which refers to a description of the skill being discussed. Next, I will tell you *why it is important.* Finally I will tell you *how to get it,* which will outline key ideas to help you develop the feel you seek.

PART ONE
The Skills

A Secure Center of Balance

What: Your physical center of balance is located in your lower abdominal area, which is the very core of your body. A horse's center of balance is located deep within his barrel behind his wither area. Your goal as a rider is to keep your center of balance

Your physical center of balance is located in your lower
abdominal area which is the very core of your body.
Your goal as a rider is to keep your center of balance in line
with your horse's.

in line with your horse's. When properly aligned you will feel connected with the horse as if an anchor has been dropped from within your center of balance directly into your horse's center of balance. You will feel stable, secure, and in control of the rest of your body.

Why it is important: How far things go astray is in direct proportion to how far a rider's center of balance is off. *There is nothing more important that you will learn in this book.* When you maintain your center of balance, your mind and body follow naturally, which will allow your horse to do his job.

How to get it: Position your seat in front of the cantle of your saddle. Rock slightly back on your seat bones. Instead of *forcing* your seat into the saddle, imagine things that evoke a feeling of softness and heavy weight in your hips and seat. Imagine that your abdomen and hips weigh 1,000 pounds. Then *allow* yourself to sink your weight softly into your horse. Imagine when you exhale that your breath drops through your abdomen, all the way into your horse's rib cage. Focus on mental images which evoke feeling. Images are powerful because they take you where you want to be automatically.

As you find your seat, do not coach yourself to *push hard* into the saddle. When you concentrate on pushing yourself down, you create stiffness and tension throughout the rest of your body. For all your efforts, you will still feel that you are on top of your saddle and not connected with your horse.

Your lower abdominal area is also the physical seat of emotional stability. That is why when you feel anxious or nervous your stomach feels upset. Likewise, when you feel calm and confident your stomach area feels warm and comfortable. Your lower abdominal area, where your center of balance is located, is the core of your physical riding, your emotions and consequently, your cutting.

When you lose your center of balance, regain it simply by bringing your awareness back to your abdomen. Repeat the steps above and focus on the feeling of being secure and easily anchored to your horse. This conscious awareness and focusing exercise will accelerate your ability to regain your center of balance.

Soft, Connected Body Alignment

What: The alignment of your entire body allows you to maintain balance, rhythm, and feel with your horse. Your shoulders should be over your hip bones. Your hip bones should be directly above your ankles. If a plumb line were dropped from your shoulders to your ankles, it would hang straight.

Why it is important: Alignment allows you to maintain your center of balance. When your body is out of alignment, your center of balance is thrown off. When your body is aligned, you feel comfortable and at ease in the saddle; you feel heavy at your center of balance; your shoulders are light, soft, and hang comfortably over your hips as your legs hang easily at your horse's sides.

How to get it: Sit in your saddle and have someone look at where your shoulders are in relationship to your hips. They should be opened naturally and seem to rest lightly over your heavy center of balance. Next, have them look to see if your legs hang comfortably below your hips. It is important to have someone else observe your body position. It is difficult to be objective, especially if you have developed poor riding habits. Also, check to make sure the

How To Find
Your Center of Balance

If you have trouble finding your center of balance on the move, try these exercises. Find your seat and center of balance while your horse is standing still. Relax and experience a soft, weighty feeling extending down into your horse. Next, feel it at a walk. As you walk, do some periodical mental checking to see if you are still in the correct seat position in your saddle. Become aware of an incorrect body position in a non-judgmental way. Simply re-adjust your seat, find your center of balance again, and breathe deeply. Allow the feel to come back. If you have to repeat this step one time or 100 times, it doesn't matter. The more you practice becoming aware of your center of balance and correcting it as necessary, the more stable your riding will become. The number of times you have to work to regain your center will dramatically decrease over time. Repeat the same technique at a trot, at a lope, or any time you are cutting. Don't become discouraged if you lose your center of balance. Just regain it softly and return to the task at hand.

fenders of your saddle are not designed to hold your legs in a constantly forward position.

Don't: Never overcompensate for long-term, poor body position habits for any length of time. For example, if you frequently end up with your legs behind you as you ride, don't overcompensate by forcing your legs way forward. You might experiment with the idea briefly to regain a comfortable, secure seat. However, if you consistently force your legs forward and keep them there, you will move your center of balance too far back, which causes tension throughout your body.

Always concentrate on the specific behavior and feel you seek. If you tend to lean too far forward, don't concentrate only on forcing your shoulders back for an extended period of time. Overcompensating is helpful only briefly while you attempt to find a new riding position. Once you find it, make sure that you stay focused on a heavy center of balance with a soft, aligned body. Work toward that goal. I cannot overemphasize this point.

A Quiet Upper Body

What: The next time you watch a cutting video of a top open or non-pro performer, focus only on that person's upper body. You will find that he or she keeps that part of their body almost motionless. In your riding, strive to achieve a quiet, motionless upper body.

How I picture the upper body is to imagine that it is a rectangle which includes my seat and shoulders but not my arms and legs. I

The entire upper body remains calm and still
no matter what else is going on.

further imagine that the bottom part of this rectangle folds and bends at the lower part of the back for stops and turns. The shoulders are open (but not forced back) and resting comfortably over the lower part of the rectangle. It feels like the lower rectangle is weighted, yet flexible. The entire upper body remains calm and still no matter what you need to do with your arms and legs. Always stay quiet no matter what your horse is doing, including trotting, loping, stopping, or turning. The upper body should naturally flow with and follow the horse's movements. It also affects how the horse slows down and stops as your lower back (the lower part of the rectangle) rounds and drops deeply into the horse. That shift in weight increases the pressure over the horse's back and signals him to slow his momentum or stop. Always strive to keep your upper body quiet, centered, and soft.

Why it is important: When your upper body is quiet and soft, and your center of balance is anchored, you have the best possible chance to be in sync with your horse. He is free to do his job. When your upper body is too far forward, your weight is displaced over the horse's front end, which makes it difficult for him to maintain his center of balance on his rear. If your upper body is too far back, again this displaces your center of balance and restricts the horse's freedom of movement. If your upper body leans to one side, you can throw the horse's balance off laterally.

How to get it: During motion and acceleration, allow the horse to take you along with his movements instead of trying to control

How To Stop Leaning

When cutters lean, it is because they are

mentally anticipating the turn. Because of

a human's inseparable connection of mind,

emotions, and body, we always show with

our bodies what's going on in our heads.

When you master keeping your upper body

quiet and soft, you will automatically gain a

sense of mental and emotional calmness,

and you will stop leaning.

him with your upper body. Think, *"quiet"* or *"still."* For decelera-
tion and stops, round your lower back and think of remaining soft,
deep, and quiet. Exhale and allow your weight to drop into the
saddle and stay there while your horse stops and turns.

Don't: Avoid affecting your horse by leaning in any direction
— laterally, forward, or backward. Focus on a quiet, soft upper
body.

Rhythmic Breathing

What: Easy, relaxed, rhythmic breathing provides oxygen to
your muscles, which in turn helps keep you relaxed and focused. It
keeps you physiologically calm by reducing your heart rate and by
reducing excessive brainwave activity. Breathing is a natural way
to regain focus and mental control. When you exhale deeply
through the core of your body, it brings your awareness back to
your center of balance.

Why it is important: Breathing is the key that opens the door
to physical, mental, and emotional control. When you hold your
breath, or take breaths that are shallow or short, you cause a chain
of negative reactions throughout your body and mind. These
negative reactions include increased muscle tension, erratic
brainwave patterns, and increased heart rate.

How to get it: Just allow air to go in and out of your body by
breathing all the way into your abdomen. Imagine exhaling down
into your horse. Concentrate on easy breathing with repetitive

Controlled eyes refers to consciously controlling your eyes to focus on the task at hand with a wide, soft field of vision.

Using soft eyes is key to mental and emotional control.

patterns of inhaling and exhaling.

Don't: Never force it. Simply allow the air into your stomach and imagine it being let out into your horse. Enjoy the relaxing effect it has on your mind and body. This exercise is particularly important during your warm-up and prior to walking into the herd.

Controlled Eyes

What: Controlled eyes refers to consciously controlling your eyes to focus on the task at hand with a wide, soft field of vision.

Why it is important: Using soft eyes is key to mental and emotional control. It allows you to make good decisions under pressure. When you see all that is in front of you, you have the necessary information to make sound decisions. You have a sense of calmness. When your vision is narrow and you look downward, you do not see all of the opportunities that surround you. That's when you tend to make rash, hasty decisions.

How to get it: Keep your chin level and your shoulders open as you practice looking forward to see what is in front of you in your wide field of vision. Take in everything you see. For an added benefit, combine looking ahead softly in the distance with rhythmic breathing.

Hinged Arms

What: Gain a feel of the separate and effective function of your arms and hands as independent extensions of your quiet upper body.

The first step is to drop your hips deep into the saddle as a signal to your horse that a reduction in speed or a stop is impending.

Next, move your rein hand forward and up to remove all the slack from the reins.

Then, slide your horn hand down the reins until you reach the horse's neck. Pull back evenly and smoothly towards your abdominal area to put pressure on the horse's mouth until you feel the horse engage his hindquarters to achieve a slow-down, stop, rock back, or turn.

Release the rein pressure.

Why it is important: The hinging action and relaxed muscle tension allow you to do what you need to do with your arms and hands while keeping your upper body quiet.

How to get it: Imagine that your arms are attached to your body by hinges at the shoulders. Practice moving them independently of your upper body whenever you ride. Your arms should feel comfortable with just the right amount of muscle tension to be responsive but not tight. Check for excessive muscle tension and relax your arms if necessary.

Don't: Never clamp your arms down at your sides, stiffen your elbows, or lean forward or backwards as you use your reins.

Two-Handed Stop

What: A two-handed stop involves using both of your hands (in practice only) to make corrections, such as a reduction of speed or a stop.

Why it is important: A two-handed stop is an effective way to return your horse to his center of balance. It is also the smoothest, most efficient way to communicate to your horse that you want him to stop softly and deeply. A two-handed stop can also help him remain on his haunches throughout a turn.

How to get it: The first step is to drop your hips (your center of balance) deep into the saddle as a signal to your horse that a reduction in speed or a stop is impending. As he learns to read your signals, he will begin to shift his weight to his rear end auto-

As a fun exercise, stop what you are doing now and look

10 to 15 feet in front of you. Focus on an object that is

directly in front of you, encompass a wide field of vision,

and at the same time, focus on your breathing. Relax.

Notice the object and all that surrounds it as you breathe

for about five seconds. Then, abruptly hold your breath.

Notice how you immediately lose your soft vision when

you stop breathing. You naturally become focused on

only that one object which lies directly in front of you.

The same thing happens when you make your cuts!

If you hold your breath, look down, and do not have the

entire picture of all the cattle in front of you, it is easy

to make poor, rash decisions. Soft eyes and breathing

go hand in hand.

matically. Next, move your rein hand forward and up to remove all the slack from the reins. Then, slide your horn hand down the reins until you reach the horse's neck. Pull back evenly and smoothly towards your abdominal area to put pressure on the horse's mouth.

When you feel the horse engage his hindquarters to achieve a slow-down, stop, rock back or turn, release the rein pressure. Pressure release is the predominate way to reward your horse and communicate to him that he has successfully completed the behavior you desire. It is imperative that you focus your attention on the feel of the reins, the horse's response, and your immediate pressure release.

Relaxed, Responsive Legs

What: Your legs should be soft, next to your horse's sides, and ready to respond instantly, when needed. Your knees should be bent at a comfortable angle. Your ankles should be directly under, and in line with, your hips.

Why it is important: Correct leg position helps you maintain your center of balance. When your legs are relaxed but ready, you can be responsive to your horse. When your leg muscles are tight, you tend to grip your horse. Gripping sends a signal to the horse to go forward as he moves away from the leg pressure. Tension in your legs often manifests itself in your horse losing his stop, rounding his turns, or leaking which is a progressive, forward

Your legs should be soft, next to your horse's sides, and ready
to respond instantly, when needed. Your knees should be bent
at a comfortable angle. Your ankles should be directly under,
and in line with, your hips. Your heels should be dropped downward, easily, but not forced down rigidly.

motion toward the cow.

How to get it: Adjust the length of your stirrups so that your knee is bent at a comfortable angle. Acquire the right feel by becoming aware of your center of balance first. Then, allow your legs to hang easily and straight underneath your hips as you drop your heels.

Make sure your stirrups aren't too short or too long. Stirrups which are too short will throw your balance forward. Stirrups that are too long cause stiffness in your legs as you reach for the stirrups and cause you to grip your horse's sides unnecessarily.

Don't: Avoid extending your legs way out in front of you in an attempt to keep your legs from going behind you. That will create increased tension in your legs which will throw your center of balance off, as well as that of your horse.

Dropped Heels

What: Your heels should be dropped downward, easily, but not forced down rigidly.

Why it is important: Your heels are key to maintaining your center of balance and keeping your legs relaxed.

How to get it: Relax and imagine dropping a plumb line from your center of balance down to your heels. Allow your mind to drop your heels easily. Sometimes repeating a key word like "drop" helps develop and enforce a physical pattern for your body to follow.

"I think the most important thing to remember while cutting is to relax your seat and legs. Let your natural balance keep you in the middle of the saddle and let the horse have as much freedom to move under you as you can give him. The idea is to let the horse do the work, and your job is simply to help."

Sandy Bonelli

Don't: Never force your heels down by extending your legs way out in front of you.

Strategic Use of Feet/Legs

What: Strategic use of your feet refers to the use of your feet and/or legs to communicate acceleration or lateral movement to your horse. It is impossible to separate the function of your feet from the function of your legs. Depending upon the sensitivity of your horse, sometimes you will use your feet via a bare heel or spurs to get a desired response. Sometimes you might only use the calves of your legs. The desired skill is to use your legs and/or feet to exert just the right amount of pressure to accelerate your horse or move him laterally.

Why it is important: Your feet and legs are critical communication tools in guiding or speeding up your horse during herdwork and while working a cow.

How to get it: Drop your heel, turn your toe slightly out, and move your leg toward your horse. Use your calf, heel, and/or spur just enough to initiate the motion you want, then instantly release the pressure. Sometimes, several short motions will get the desired response. If you have trouble using your legs, sit in your saddle while it is on a saddle stand. Imagine that your knees and ankles are free to turn your toe out and move your leg/foot laterally, making contact with your horse's side.

Don't: Never hold leg or heel/spur pressure continuously into

"A good horse is very sensitive to a rider's body messages. If these messages are consistent, the comfort level of the horse is consistent with the message. If I think stop, my body sends this message to the horse through the effective use of my seat. This is true with the hands, legs, etc."

Mary Jo Milner

your horse's side.

PART TWO
Basic Warm-up Maneuvers Outside the Herd

Feel for the Stop

What: Developing feel for the stop is a systematic way of using your seat to communicate to the horse your intention to stop.

Why it is important: The steps outlined below allow a horse to make his own decision to stop in response to your seat which results in an immediate soft, folding motion. When the horse understands and recognizes a signal executed during the warm-up procedure, it carries over into the cutting arena. The desired effect is an ability to ask your horse to stop at any speed, in or out of the herd, by merely giving him a signal with your seat position.

How to get it: Prior to actually stopping your horse, mentally prepare yourself for the following steps. Focus. Relax. Give yourself plenty of time to execute the steps without being in a hurry to stop. Drop your weight into your horse by exhaling and focusing on dropping your center of balance into your horse as you round your lower back. If your horse does not understand this communication, allow him to feel your body sink into him without picking up on the reins for at least three or four strides. If your horse does not slow his speed or stop on his own, smoothly help him by executing a two-handed stop. Then, back a few steps.

"The 'art' of riding a cutting horse is to sit on your pockets balanced without having your legs stiff. Move from your waist down, without moving your top half."

Lindy Burch

Next, let him stand still and totally relax until he exhales. Wait until he is so relaxed that he does not move forward until you ask him to move. This approach will cause your horse to want to stop and to stop softly and deeply on his hindquarters.

Don't: Avoid forcing your horse to stop abruptly by suddenly jerking up on the reins. After you have stopped, don't move him forward without first allowing him to settle and relax.

The Backup

What: While backing up, a horse should move several steps backwards with his back rounded, and his poll slightly flexed. His mouth should feel soft and responsive and the backward motion should feel effortless.

Why it is important: A horse rocking back on his hindquarters is an all-important aspect of the stop/turn sequence executed by your horse while working a cow (discussed further in Chapter 6). The horse stops (first step), rocks back on his hindquarters (second step), then holds that balance point as he turns. Backing a horse builds strength in the horse's hindquarters as well as an understanding of that request when you school him while working a cow. When your horse backs easily and is responsive to bit pressure, you know you are communicating with your horse without resistance.

How to get it: Use the same hand positions as described for a two-handed stop. Pull evenly and smoothly on the reins with your

Direct Reining Maneuver

right hand and ask the horse to move back. Ask for more distance, responsiveness, and quickness from the horse in small increments. Always reward a correct response by immediately releasing the bit pressure.

Don't: Never approach this maneuver unfocused, i.e., being unaware of how forcefully you pull and being unaware of your horse's response.

Head/Neck Flexibility

What: A flexible horse is one who has supple neck muscles and who will bring his nose toward your leg with a direct rein pull.

Why it is important: Many training methods utilize a direct rein cue after a stop to guide a horse through the cutting turn. When a horse flexes by giving his nose, he is willing and responsive.

How to get it: Ask the horse to give to a direct rein cue by applying even pressure with the rein and holding it. Immediately release the rein pressure when the horse gives his nose in response to your request. Gradually increase the amount of flexion as your horse comes to understand the signal until you gain your desired response.

Don't: Never flex the horse by jerking or forcefully pulling on the rein. Just wait for the horse to respond and, when he does, reward him by releasing the pressure.

Neck Reining Maneuver

Neck Reining

What: Neck reining is achieved when a horse moves in a direction (left, for example) by responding to pressure applied on the opposite side of his neck (right).

Why it is important: It is important because a horse that doesn't neck rein may have problems changing directions quickly as he maneuvers through the herd for cuts.

How to get it: This topic is too lengthy for me to summarize here. I will simply say that a horse should be taught to respond to direct rein pressure as well as to neck reining. Because young cutting horses are often trained to turn using direct rein signals, problems may occur in shows when you attempt to neck rein while making the cut. For example, say you neck rein your horse and your intended direction is left. Instead of responding quickly, he sticks his nose out to the right. This happens because he is relying on direct rein pressure to direct his movement.

If you are having problems with neck reining during cuts, consult a professional trainer to help you and your horse master this skill. It is essential that you feel totally confident as you maneuver your horse through the herd.

Now that you understand how to develop key basic riding skills, it's time to learn essential mental and emotional skills for our sport.

The mental and emotional ability to perform under pressure is a skill to be understood, learned, and practiced, just like learning to cut. This chapter explains those skills and shows you how to acquire them.

"It's never over till it's over. Never stop fighting. Never
give up. Never surrender. No matter how bad it gets, no
matter how deep your pain; persistence, faith in yourself,
and an undauntable spirit will eventually break you free."

Jim Loehr, Ed. D.

CHAPTER 5

LEARN THE MENTAL SKILLS OF GREAT COMPETITORS

Since the beginning of my career as a cutting horse trainer, I
have noticed certain riders—professional and non-professional—
who rode horses that have minimal talent and skill; yet, they made
it to the finals of major events. I also saw others who rode very
talented horses but performed inconsistently. I knew something
powerful was going on. That was when I first began to study the
mental side of our sport. I had to find out what that special something was.

For the past 20 years, a team of professionals,

including a sport psychologist, an exercise physi-

ologist, a nutritionist, a sports medicine physi-

cian, and a psychonueroimmunologist, has stud-

ied what makes people perform at their best

under pressure. After extensive research with

both Olympic and professional athletes, they

created Mentally Tough, a program for all ath-

letes and performers, including cutters. It incor-

porates training for the entire person—mind,

body, and emotions. Dr. Loehr, pioneer of the

Mentally Tough program, and the entire LGE

Sport Science Inc. staff in Orlando, Florida, have

combined their expertise to continually develop

and perfect Mentally Tough concepts which can

be applied to all sports, as well as to daily living.

In 1985, my sister, Tootie Lyons, heard Dr. Jim Loehr speak on a radio talk show about Mentally Tough® Training. I searched bookstores and found a copy of his early book *Mental Toughness Training for Sports*. That book became my personal mental and emotional training guide. The lessons I learned from Dr. Loehr's program have played a key role in my success as a cutter. Mentally Tough skills are powerful, and they work.

I had many horses in training from 1982 until 1994. I first began to make the Mentally Tough program a part of my personal showing skills in 1985. In 1994, I decided to seek out Dr. Loehr personally and become more thoroughly acquainted with his program.

My timing couldn't have been better. Dr. Loehr wanted to certify instructors for the Mentally Tough program in specific sports. In 1995, I became the first person licensed to teach the Mentally Tough skills outside of the immediate staff members of LGE. I now teach the LGE principles to equestrians in all disciplines. My goal is to teach people how to optimize their personal talents and skills in any situation by harnessing the collective powers of their mind, their body, and their emotions.

Every sport has its unique mental and/or emotional challenges.

"You need to relax your mind before entering the herd. Take plenty of time."

L.H. Wood

As a cutting competitor, you are faced with many variables that are out of your direct control. The herd. Your help. Your horse. But somehow the challenge of being responsive, moment to moment, to an ever-changing situation is what makes cutting exciting and unique. Controlling your mind and your emotions is key to being able to make split-second decisions.

Why Train Mentally and Emotionally?

I consistently see cutters, both professional and non-professional, who lack confidence and who do not believe in themselves. Some stop having fun and lose their passion.

Sometimes the difficulties that precede a show seem insurmountable. Cutting can suddenly be miserable if you didn't perform well in practice, had a rift with a trainer or client, received outside negative comments about your horse, or drew up late in a bad group of cattle. Instead of the difficulties adding up to a challenge, they seem to be a direct attack on your self-esteem as a cutter and, sometimes, as a person. Cutting is supposed to be fun!

The Mentally Tough program can give you concrete strategies to help you perform at your highest levels no matter what the situation. It will also help you derive more fun and joy from the

The Ideal Performance State (IPS) or feeling in the zone, is a combination of many positive emotions (calm, confident, energized, focused, having fun, relaxed, and ready) happening simultaneously. You don't just feel energized or just feel calm or just feel focused—you feel a combination of high, positive emotion all at once. That is what makes IPS unique and powerful.

entire process. The program is based on achieving a balance of mind, body, and emotion. The hallmark of the program's success lies in being able to call up feelings associated with the highest possible positive emotions to achieve the Ideal Performance State[SM] (IPS). Others describe IPS as being "in the zone."

When you are experiencing IPS you feel confident, challenged, energetic, focused, relaxed, and ready to perform without feeling nervous, stressed, or anxious. You know how to block out distractions when you enter a show, or any stressful situation, so that anyone or anything negative will not affect your level of performance. A rider trained in Mentally Tough principles can perform in the show arena at their highest levels . . . and not leave their best efforts in the practice pen.

Why is IPS Important?

Talent is inherited, God-given. Skill is acquired. For example, technical cutting skills are learned through understanding and practice. Although some riders might be talented athletically for riding, all must learn the numerous dimensions of our sport. Then, as those physical skills are acquired, they are demonstrated in an orchestrated situation—a show, for example. It is in the show

"This is where you will win the battle — in the playhouse of your mind."

Maxwell Maltz

arena that I used to think my favorite cutting heroes had some special God-given talent to be able to cut and ride so magnificently when the heat was on. I also thought that when God created me he said, "Okay, Barb, all your buddies are gifted as show men and women in cutting. And I have also given you special gifts. You can fry terrific eggs and you have great kitchen cleaning skills!" I really thought I had been shorted! Then, as I studied Mentally Tough concepts, I was relieved to discover that the mental and emotional ability to perform under pressure is a SKILL to be understood, learned, and practiced, just like learning to cut. I was elated! It was wonderful news. If I wanted to be a great performer at cutting, or anything else, I just had to learn how.

I hope you are relieved, too. If you don't keep it together and ride at your best when it means the most to you, relax. This chapter will show you how. Then, it's up to you to practice. This training can give you a powerful competitive edge, no matter your class level. But you must follow through by taking action.

From a Physical Viewpoint

Sometimes people say to me, "All of that mental and emotional training stuff is bunk! Just keep cutting long enough and

"If you think you can or can't, you're right."

John Paxton

you'll get it." Obviously, I disagree with that philosophy. I do agree that there is no substitute for experience. But you can <u>learn</u> to maximize your experiences as you go and take the shortest road possible to successful showing.

It is vital to understand that positive and negative emotional states are reflected in your body by muscle tension, brain wave frequency, blood pressure, and heart rate. Thinking is an electro-chemical event in the brain and, therefore, is physical. Emotions are neurochemical and, therefore, are physical.

Whether you are a beginner or a veteran cutter, when you feel positive emotions, your brain waves have a specific, even pattern, your muscles are more relaxed, and your vision is softer and broader. Your body is just right to perform well. Therefore, when you are experiencing IPS, you have the potential to ride to your best talent and skill levels from a physical standpoint. When you are feeling negative, you can perform at some level, but it won't be your best because your body is affected.

When you feel negative (it doesn't matter why, there are millions of reasons) and you ride, your body chemistry physically blocks your performance. Your muscles are tight. Your brain-wave patterns are erratic, which means you can't think clearly.

Toughness Training Model

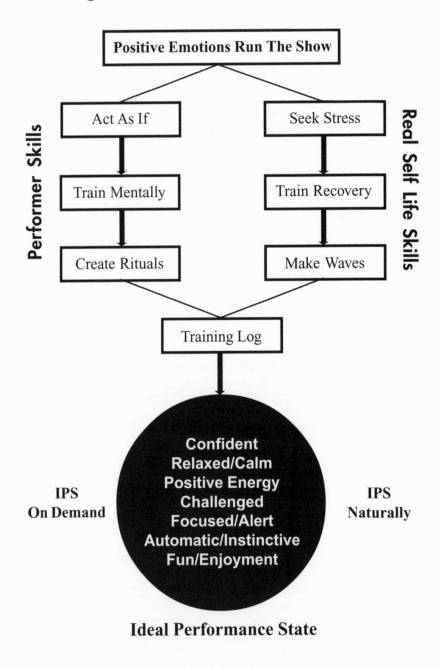

Your heart feels as if it is about to pound right out of your chest. And, your field of vision is narrow. Except by pure luck, you couldn't see the best cow to cut if it was standing in front of you yelling, "Hey! I'm it. Cut me!"

What we seek, then, is the ability to <u>control</u> IPS. The capacity to call up high, positive emotions on demand is what allows your personal talent and skill to come to life when you need it most. If you don't think that you can feel the emotions of IPS in any situation, it is only because you have not learned or practiced how to call up those feelings. If you learn and practice this program, it will add more joy and more personal challenge to your cutting. Acquiring the ability to get into IPS on demand is a skill. You learn it the same way you learn any other skill. You understand what it is, why it's important, and how to do it. The more committed you are to practicing, the more skilled you will become. The extra-special bonus is that these ways of thinking and acting will benefit every aspect of your daily life, as well. That is my favorite part about this whole experience. Here are six steps to help you anchor yourself in powerful positive emotions.

"I image a run before I start to the herd. Then, after I start the run , I stay focused on the business at hand."

Gil Porter

Step #1: *Create a Grand Vision of Your Cutting*

Mastering the performance skills necessary to experience IPS begins with a dream. Create in your mind the type of cutter you want to become by dreaming a cutting dream that excites you. There are no limits. Create, in detail, the controlled, confident, focused rider that you want to become. Think it through thoroughly.

So, here is your assignment. Sit in a comfortable position. Close your eyes. Let go of all the weaknesses you now have and create a moving picture in your mind of the rider you would like to become. If you have trouble getting a clear picture in your mind, think of a rider whom you admire. See that person in your mind and imagine that the image you see is you. Watch a video of another rider if that helps. You can even combine images of different riders to create your own unique style. Then, carve that image indelibly into your mind.

Take the time to write out your description. Be specific. Write the following words: graceful, assertive, calm, or whatever words give you the feeling and look you want to achieve. Read your description often. When you read it aloud, it should excite you.

This step is crucial because it forces you to decide exactly what

Mental and Emotional Awareness Worksheet

Disempowering Feeling	Where/ When	Positive Emotion Replacement
Days before show		
_____	_____	_____
_____	_____	_____
_____	_____	_____
_____	_____	_____
_____	_____	_____
Day of the show		
_____	_____	_____
_____	_____	_____
_____	_____	_____
_____	_____	_____
_____	_____	_____
While showing		
_____	_____	_____
_____	_____	_____
_____	_____	_____
_____	_____	_____
_____	_____	_____

you want to achieve and how you want to ride. Then, your subconscious goes to work to bring reality into line with the image you have in your mind. Without the picture, your riding will be scattered and without a clear destination. As you learn more with time, embellish the picture to make it even better. This step is often overlooked by many cutters. However, taking the time to create a powerful self-image as a strong cutter, and using it to excite you every day, is as important as anything you will ever do in your cutting career.

Step #2: *Establish a Training Starting Point*

Because gaining emotional control is a skill, you start at some specific point and improve from there. It's exactly like learning any other skill. You become aware of your mental and emotional riding strengths and weaknesses. Then you go to work, systematically improving your weakest areas.

Here is how you do it. Refer to the Mental and Emotional Awareness Worksheet. The headlines across the top of the page have the following meanings. <u>Disempowering feeling</u> refers to any negative feeling that weakens your sense of confidence and power from within; i.e., anger, frustration, nervousness, etc. <u>When/where</u> refers to when or where it occurs; i.e., while practicing and your

How To Eliminate
Negative Thoughts

The concept of replacement is a key to achieving mental,

emotional, or technical skills. Once you have objectively

evaluated where your weaknesses are, shift your focus to

achieving what you want. Eliminate negative thoughts and

words which dwell on what you don't want. Instead,

replace the negative with the positive. "Don't get

nervous," becomes "Relax." "Don't fall back," becomes

"Stay up." "Don't lean," becomes "Stay soft and quiet."

Instead of unconsciously reinforcing what you're trying

to avoid, empower yourself with what you desire.

horse misses, before you ride into the herd, etc. <u>Positive replace-</u>
<u>ment</u> refers to what emotion would instead empower in that same
situation; i.e., confident, calm, focused, etc. The left side of the
page is divided into three sections vertically with the following
headings. <u>Days before show</u> refers to the days, weeks, or months
before the actual day you ride (practicing); <u>Day of the show</u> refers
to the time from when you wake up on show day until you enter
the arena; and <u>While showing</u> refers to the time you are competing.

Now, pinpoint any negative feelings in the first time-frame,
such as nervousness, fear, anxiousness, anger, defensiveness,
feeling distracted, within the times they occur in practice or anytime before the actual day of the show. Reflect on exactly when
and where that specific feeling happens, like practicing in front of
others or when you pull into the show grounds. Identifying exactly
what you feel, and when, is critical. It is at those times that you
will target your training.

Do this same exercise for the next two time segments. Then,
in the positive replacement column, identify the wonderful feeling
you would prefer to experience. This is a critical step because you
will concentrate your efforts on conditioning those positive emotions. Remember this important point: <u>you can never get rid of any</u>

"We have all been taught to believe that negative equals realistic and positive equals unrealistic. To live a creative life, we must lose our fear of being wrong."

Joseph Chilton Pearce

<u>negative feeling by wanting to get rid of it</u>. You must identify the positive replacement and then train for it as you would train to perfect any other skill. Feeling confident, no matter what, is a skill!

This awareness process allows you to get in touch with your disempowering feelings as well as identify when and where they happen. You can then identify how you want to feel so that you can train yourself to respond positively instead of negatively.

Once you have clear ideas about what you wish to create in your riding (Step 1), what your current skill level is and what you want to feel (Step 2), the next step is to practice being able to feel powerful, positive emotions on demand.

Mental, physical, and emotional states are not disconnected from one another—they are one. Because of this mind, body, and emotional oneness, you can gain emotional control (IPS) by what you do with your body (physical) and what you do with your mind (mental). These are called performer skills. We will explore the physical or acting aspects of performer skills first.

Step #3: *Train From the Outside-In With Acting Skills*

Whatever you do with your body on the outside, connects to different emotional states on the inside. For example, the physiology of sadness is slumped shoulders, downward eyes, drawn facial

"A person needs to look and act confident."

Paul Hansma

muscles, turned-down mouth, and shallow breathing. Obviously, the physiology of fun and joy is the opposite. A major break-through in learning to control your emotions is to understand that you can go a long way towards acquiring a positive mindset by simply controlling your body.

Most of us just show on the outside exactly the way we feel on the inside. From now on, instead of being at the mercy of your emotions, you can, instead, learn to control your emotions by controlling your body. When you train on the outside, you auto-matically train on the inside. By conditioning your body to "act" like a calm, confident, successful cutter, you take a giant step in becoming that rider within.

If you really feel tired, nervous, rushed, or angry, do you let it show in the arena? A bad actor and someone unskilled in IPS will. But, if you are skilled in acting, you live by the cardinal rule—never show any negative emotion on the outside. Signal loud and clear with your body that you love being right where you are despite the pressure and no matter the chaos. There are three powerful techniques to keep the chaos that surrounds you from affecting you in the arena: concentrate on your posture, focus on where your eyes are directed, and control your breathing.

When you keep your eyes up and your focus wide, soft, and scanning, your mind will stay focused on what you want to accomplish.

Acting Skill #1: Posture Control

We are conditioned to believe that we can act confident only after we've earned that right through some grandiose accomplishment. But acting confident, relaxed, and focused no matter what you really feel will access high, positive emotions within. You might really feel nervous at some point, but by controlling your posture, you control your emotions. Posture control means keeping your chin up and your shoulders open. Prior to entering the herd, or whenever you feel weak, walk or sit in the saddle with your shoulders back and chin up.

Acting Skill #2: Eye Control

Controlling your eyes controls your emotions because your mind naturally follows your eyes. When you are anxious or nervous, your eyes naturally go down and your vision narrows. The effect feels like a vice closing in on your head with side blinders. But, when you keep your eyes up and your focus wide, soft, and scanning, no matter how you really feel, your mind will stay focused on what you want to accomplish. You will feel calmer and be able to actually see all the options. Plan where your eyes will be, moment to moment, in your run as carefully as you plan anything else. For example, your eyes are soft and looking to the

The Cardinal Rule of Acting

No matter what's really happening

inside or around you;

NEVER SHOW WEAKNESS ON

THE OUTSIDE.

middle of the arena as you scan the cattle for your cut. As you work the cow, your eyes remain softly focused on the cow's neck or head.

Acting Skill #3: Controlled Breathing

Controlling your breathing accomplishes three things at once. First, it slows your brain wave activity which allows you to think clearly. Then, it increases the oxygen flow to the muscles throughout your body which relaxes them. Third, it provides a natural internal focus which calms you and helps you concentrate. Whenever you become aware of any negative emotions, start breathing all the way into your abdomen. Inhale slowly and deeply. Let your tummy expand like a balloon. Let it fall as you exhale slowly. Make the exhalation cycle longer than the inhalation or exhale twice before you inhale again. Then, get into a comfortable breathing rhythm. Do as many repetitions as you like. You will become calmer and more focused with each repetition.

Step #4: *Train From the Inside-Out With Mental Conditioning*

In striving to reach the goal of calling up positive emotions (calm, confident, focused, relaxed or energized) on demand, the next powerful approach is through what you do with your mind.

"Think forward, not back. Keep your thoughts confined to the moment at hand. People go wrong by thinking of scores to beat, what the event is, who's looking, what happened a second before, etc."

Helen Groves

After you practice and become skilled in the following mental conditioning techniques, combine them with the acting tools.

Mental Conditioning Tool #1: Scripting

The first mental conditioning tool to achieve emotional control is scripting. Scripting refers to what you say to yourself, either planned or spontaneous. If we have not become skilled mentally and emotionally, we tend to talk to ourselves about what we fear and what we don't want to happen. Scripting, on the other hand, is about always talking to yourself in strong, positive words about what you want to happen technically, as well as mentally and emotionally. One way to help you control your thoughts is to pretend that you have the best, most positive coach in the world, or an angel, sitting on your shoulder telling you exactly what to do.

Plan some key words and phrases to use at specific times. For example, talk to yourself during your warm up. Tell yourself to relax and breathe. When you're not really feeling relaxed, this will help—especially when you combine this skill with acting skills. Keep in mind that the intensity of emotion can flow in both directions. Sometimes, instead of needing to calm ourselves down, we may need to rise to the occasion, especially if it is late in the day or if you have already had a bad run. You might need to remind

"The mental aspect is one of the biggest priorities, if not the biggest, to becoming a winner. A person can work his butt off and do his homework, but if his mental game is not correct, all the hard work goes down the drain."

Dick Cogdell

yourself to "stay gritty, stay tough, come on, get going."

In your warm up and as you walk to the herd, it is easy to talk to yourself in words, phrases, and sentences. But when you make the turn in the herd and walk up for the cut, things begin to happen quickly. Thinking now must be instinctive, instead of analytical. Even so, there are still key words and phrases that can keep you grounded in the moment. For example, you might remind yourself to "step up" or "breathe" or "look at the top." Pick out a word or phrase that will help you stay focused on what you need to work on the most. Rely on yourself instead of others. Then, once you put your hand down, tell yourself "ride to the neck" or "stay soft." Remember to focus on things you want to happen, not on those you don't want. Your script or key words should be personal and based on your needs. Whatever works when you say it to yourself . . . go for that.

Strong, positive words and self-coaching spontaneously is also crucial. For example, as you walk through the herd you may be searching for the good cattle you picked out earlier. But, at that moment, they are absolutely no where to be found! Flexibility in situations that are different than you had planned will separate you mentally, emotionally, and physically from other cutters. Be your

"Visualization, no substitute for it! Your visualization skills are a big step in preparing for an event."

Carole Thorsnes

own best coach. When things seem to be getting out of control, tell yourself: "Stay cool." "Just wait." "It'll work out." Breathe, trust the moment, and you'll most often make the right decision.

Mental Conditioning Tool #2: Imaging

Mental imaging or the ability to visualize is one of the most powerful mental conditioning tools you can use. A picture is worth a thousand words in taking you where you want to go. As you fill your mind with images of yourself as the cutter you will be during your next run, make sure you combine the images with emotion; i.e., intensity, focus, confidence, and calmness. Once this image has been created in your mind, your brain automatically begins to program your subconscious to bring that image into reality. You actually become what you imagine—both good and bad. So be careful!!

A high level of visualization is the ability to see clear mental pictures of your great performance any time, under any condition. You can either call up the entire run you have imagined or only a tiny portion of it. You decide what you need according to the situation. For example, say you have just watched five cutters work. Three lost cattle, one back fenced, and the other's horse ran off. If you are untrained mentally and emotionally, you would

"Don't fear anything you cannot control. Always be determined. People sometimes make the mistake of being impatience, then try to make it happen instead of letting it happen."

Kobie Wood

imagine the same things happening to you. But if you are skilled

mentally, you would focus on your job, i.e., specifically with what

you need to do to put your run together. See yourself staying cool

and making great decisions in tough situations. As those things

consume your mind, you have the best chance for a positive out-

come in the most difficult situation.

Mental Conditioning Tool #3: Power Questions

"What's my job?" and "What do I have control of?"

Both of those questions help you stay focused on your job.

Consider this. As a cutter, all you have is yourself, your horse, and

2 1/2 minutes per run to make two or three cuts and work two or

three cattle. That's it! Everything else—the outcome of the run,

the noise in the stands, the judge, the ground, the people around

you making comments—is out of your control. Concerning your-

self with any of that is wasted energy that undermines your poten-

tial and it is not your job.

Your job is to get yourself ready, get your horse ready, and go

through a run relaxed, aggressive, and focused moment to moment.

When distractions occur, ask yourself the two questions, "What is

my job?" and "What do I have control of?" That will force you to

re-focus. You will do your job at your highest level while other

"I try to remind myself that the moment may seem important, but it's not the end of the world if things don't go right."

Spencer Harden

people and things over which you have no control will not affect you.

Mental Conditioning Tool #4: Power Phrases

"No Problem" and "Next Time"

One of the most important performer skills is the ability to stay in the moment. Our natural tendency, however, is to worry about the past or the future. Here's a tip to help you stay in the moment during your run. No matter if you make a major error or a tiny one, say to yourself "no problem." That phrase keeps you from replaying the error over and over again in your mind. It keeps you on target. Then, ask yourself what you will do "next time." This technique lets you replace what didn't work with what will work so you can do it correctly the next time the opportunity presents itself. It also affirms a belief in yourself that you can do it.

Mental Conditioning Tool #5: The Challenge Response

This fifth mental conditioning tool is one of my favorites. As Murphy's Law proves, at certain times, everything can fall apart. For cutting it can be anything from a horse throwing a shoe just prior to your turn to not having enough warm-up time, to drawing up last, to realizing a helper is missing at the last moment. People untrained in thinking skills who meet adversity tend to respond in

"Do or do not.
There is no try."

Yoda

a negative or defensive manner. But when high level competitors are faced with adversity, they will immediately search for solutions to problems or will place the problem aside if nothing can be done. They understand that difficulties are part of the game, and they view them as challenges. Many world-class competitors who are trained in mental and emotional skills learn to welcome the tough times. It is as if they say, "Give me more. I love this. I can handle it!" They do not dread difficulties but welcome them. They see that feeling challenged and rising to the occasion is what separates them from the rest. Adversity is a true test of your strengths and abilities.

Step #5: *Establish World Class Rituals*

Another important aspect of the Mentally Tough program that can help you remain calm and focused is the use of a consistent ritual prior to your run. Rituals are habitual ways of thinking and acting. Rituals combine thinking and acting skills to call up positive feelings in an instant. They can be physical, mental, or both. An example would be backing your horse, opening your shoulders, pulling your hat down and saying, "I'm ready" to yourself just prior to walking to the herd. Other examples would be tightening your saddle three riders before your turn, reminding

"I think a horse can sense how you feel. It's important to stay positive."

Mitch Farris

yourself of the cattle you like, and saying, "stay cool" to yourself.

Rituals serve as anchors of positive emotion which help prepare you to do your best. They are extremely personal. What
works for you may not work for anyone else. What is important is
that you figure out what does work for you and condition the
ritual's association with feelings of calmness, confidence, and
assertiveness. Be sure to use your ritual no matter how hectic
things may get. Develop your own ritual, and make it highly
personal. It will ensure that you stay calm and focused as you
begin your run.

Step #6: *Recovery*

A skill that separates top competitors from others is their
ability to relax or recover between cattle. The ability to train
yourself to relax in the several seconds that elapses after you have
quit your cow before you re-enter the herd is as important as
anything else you do to keep yourself grounded within your run.

Here's an example of how it works. Quit the cow with smooth
hand motions. When you control your body you control your
mind. Look at the cow briefly as you quit. Remember, eye control
also controls your mind and emotions. Next, turn your horse
around in an easy manner. In the moments following the turn-

"Far better it is to dare mighty things, to win glorious triumphs, even though checkered by failure, than to rank with those poor spirits who neither enjoy much nor suffer much, because they live in the gray twilight that knows not victory nor defeat."

Theodore Roosevelt

around, hesitate for a second or two. Take a deep breath and tell yourself to relax. You have just reduced your heart rate and brain-wave activity which will allow you to make good decisions on your next cut. Then, look for your cattle and strategize how aggressive you need to be on this cut depending on how your run has unfolded so far. The time between cattle is important for you to decide how to build your run, especially if you had a miss or a cow ran through the turn-back men, or whatever.

Design Your Own Constant Improvement Program

We never stop growing or learning. No one ever makes it to a place where there is nothing more to learn. I express my love for horses and riding through cutting. Although I have been fortunate to achieve some success, it is my hope that I have only touched the tip of the iceberg for internal and external achievements.

Like tools in a toolbox, the skills described in this chapter are there when you need them. Try them out. See what works for you. For example, if you are feeling anxious or nervous prior to your run, focus on your breathing and mentally rehearse how you will make your cuts and how you will ride your horse. If you begin to feel anxious as the cattle walk up for the cut, concentrate on

"As in any sport, confidence is the key. When you ride to the herd, you must believe you are ready so you can relax and let your mind work to its best ability.

When I ride to the herd, I want to feel like my horse is ready and all I have to concentrate on are my cattle. I think beginners get bogged down with the little worries about which leg to kick with and if the horse will roll up the pen.

Enter the herd believing you are ready and your only job is to cut the right cows."

Sandy Bonelli

watching the cattle on the outside and near the end of the flow so that you will see the best options available. None of us ever fully arrive. We are simply on our own paths of experience. My path is not your path. Yours is not mine. The secret is to learn to enjoy where you are now and make striving for excellence fun. If you make a commitment to learn and practice the fundamentals of mental and emotional control, you will discover more joy, fun, calmness, and confidence in your cutting and in your life.

Now that you have identified your goals, have a good horse, built a strong support system, developed basic riding skills, and are working toward mental and emotional control for cutting, you are in the ideal state of preparation to practice the technical aspects of riding a trained horse and working a cow.

This chapter explains the basic principles of

riding a trained cutting horse while working a

cow. It includes a discussion of the basic form of

a cutting turn, positioning on the cow, as well as

rhythm and synchronism while working a cow.

"Have as much cow savvy as the horse. Know the position to be in to keep the cow from returning to the herd. Make cutting as simple as possible."

Paul Hansma

CHAPTER 6

RIDE YOUR TRAINED HORSE EFFECTIVELY

It's vital that you have a mental picture of the correctness and form of a trained cutting horse. The first part of this chapter will help you understand what you want your horse to do . . . period. It is not a discussion of what you do to affect your horse's behavior. I will help you create a vision of rhythmic, smooth, graceful cutting runs where horse and rider work as partners. With that clear mental image, you will find it easier to automatically guide your hands, your seat, your legs and feet to achieve the position, rhythm, and poise you seek. Without a clear picture, it is easy to focus on all that is wrong and create more of the same.

"Know your horse. Learn enough to support him when necessary and stay out of his way when he doesn't need support."

Dick Gaines

The second part of this chapter is more analytical. It identifies exactly how your upper body, seat, legs, and feet aid or distract a trained cutting horse. It is about understanding how to use your body to achieve the ideal cutting picture you have created. This chapter is not about schooling a horse. We will talk about that in detail in Chapter Seven.

Create A Mental Image of Excellence, Poise, Grit, and Style

Step #1: *Define your job in the show arena*

It is easy to think that the job of a cutting horse, in traditional terms, is to be defensive and prevent the cow from returning to the herd. Today, however, showing cutting horses is about being offensive. It is about presenting your horse's talents and abilities in the best manner possible—in the middle of the pen, holding a line, controlling the cow, and basically telegraphing to the judge, "We are here. We are confident. We are going to show you our uniqueness, and it is great!" The job of a cutting horse and its rider is to paint a picture of excellence, grit, desire, and style all within a framework of correct form, motion, and rhythm.

Step #2: *Ride to maintain a horse's center of balance on its hindquarters*

I believe that a horse must maintain his center of balance when working just as you must maintain yours while riding. Every moment that a cutting horse is working a cow, the horse's balance

Every moment that a cutting horse is working a cow, the horse's balance should either be centered over its hindquarters or getting ready to shift to the hindquarters.

should either be centered over its hindquarters or getting ready to shift to the hindquarters. This applies to all situations, from standing still to traveling across the arena to stopping and turning with the cow. Even when you are on the ends, or the cow is stopped anywhere in front of you, it should feel as if your horse is rocked back and ready to initiate the next move. For stops and turns, a horse bends his hocks, keeps his weight over his hindquarters, rocks back even more on his hindquarters as he turns, and then accelerates using his rear to drive forward.

When you are first learning to cut, it is easy to be unaware of whether or not your horse is on his rear because you are preoccupied with other things, such as holding your line, traveling to the ends, sitting quietly, or not losing a cow. However, as you gain experience you will learn to ride to help your horse maintain his center of balance, moment to moment. Then, many other things will naturally fall into place. Control of a horse's center of balance means control of his physical maneuvers. With physical control comes mental control for both you and your horse.

As a general guideline to enhance "feel," you will know if your horse is balanced and working off his hindquarters when you feel as if he could make the next move or put on his brakes effortlessly at any moment. He should feel controlled and ready for what's to come.

Step #3: *Ride in rhythm with the basic form of a cutting turn*
The cutting turn is one of the primary things that makes our

"Go with the
horse on the
line and stop.
Let him carry
you through the
turn."

Keith Barnett

sport exhilarating. Your goal is to understand the individual parts of a turn and then experience those parts in a rhythmic pattern in unison with the cow. When that happens, cutting becomes much more than just analytical movements. You'll have arrived at a place where your cuts flow and where working a cow becomes a rhythm which is the essence of cutting. Conversely, if the turn loses its form and rhythm, whatever follows will feel out of control, chaotic, or panicky.

Your horse's moves should be determined by what the cow does. Much like a tennis match, players move according to the motion of the ball. In cutting, the horse and rider move in a rhythmic response to the cow. But in tennis, you lose immediately if you don't keep your eye on the ball and respond to it. Cutting is unlike tennis in that it is possible to move in the general vicinity of a cow without good form and rhythm and still manage to hold a cow or complete a run. Cutting then becomes exquisite when you achieve the perfect balance between correct form, rhythm of movement, and control of the cow.

Step #4:   *Stop and turn in correct form*

The stop and turn in cutting can be described in five steps. To begin the sequence, I'll set the stage. Imagine that you have already cut a cow from the herd, and you and your horse are moving in a parallel position with the cow across the arena. As your horse moves, he is driving forward from his rear end. This allows him to stop at any moment because his weight is already shifted to his hindquarters.

Just prior to the turn, your horse rocks back. You and your
horse stay physically and mentally controlled,
waiting for the cow to make the next move.

1. ***Get to the bottom of the stop.***

   When the cow stops at any place in the arena, your
   horse stops, bends his hocks, and rounds his back.
   There is a feeling of completion, depth, and hold in the
   stop. Your horse's rear end is engaged and ready for
   the next move.

2. ***Rock back just prior to the turn.***

   When your horse is squarely anchored on his rear end,
   which is the most physically-controlled position for a
   turn, his shoulders and rib cage ideally are lined up
   with his hindquarters. His body is collected, which
   means his weight is balanced over his rear. Then, there
   is another rock-back motion when your horse feels as if
   he gets even deeper into the ground. (Thus far in our
   discussion, the cow hasn't moved.) This rocked-back
   time, anywhere from a milli-second to moments, is a
   basic element in the turn's rhythm. This is the place
   where you and your horse must stay physically and
   mentally controlled, waiting for the cow to make the
   next move. In the prettiest of cutting turns, your horse
   melts softly into his stops, and then rocks back in
   preparation for a controlled turn.

3. ***Remain in control throughout the turn.***

   In the step above, your horse is waiting to turn as he is
   rocked back on his rear. The next step, the actual turn,

How far your horse rotates as he turns, and when and from where he accelerates, determines where he will end up strides later.

A horse that does not complete the turn and accelerates too quickly will come out toward the cow.

Ideally, the horse should accelerate at approximately the 150- to 170- degree point in the turn.

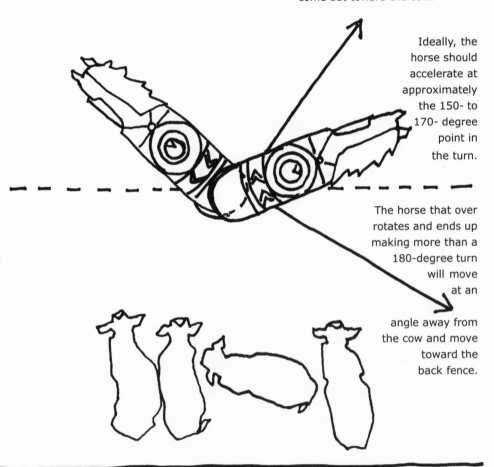

The horse that over rotates and ends up making more than a 180-degree turn will move at an

angle away from the cow and move toward the back fence.

is always initiated by the cow. As the horse's body remains controlled, his nose comes first in the direction of the turn. Then, his rear end swivels as his front end pushes off and moves across his hindquarters.

To help you gain the feel of a controlled turn, become aware when you and your horse are softly anchored behind as the horse's front end moves across his rear end. The horse's front end should move cleanly, without taking extra steps and shifting his weight forward onto his front end. After the cow moves, your horse turns almost as if being pulled through the turn by the cow. The speed of the turn directly correlates with the speed of the cow. Your horse mirrors the cow's moves in a rhythm similar to one dance partner following another. The leader of a dance pair initiates the move, but the partner instantly follows in rhythm. So it is with cow and horse.

4. *After the turn, accelerate at the appropriate angle.* How far your horse rotates as he turns, and when and where he accelerates from, determines where he will end up strides later. For example, a horse that does not complete the turn and accelerates too quickly will come out toward the cow. The horse that over rotates and ends up making more than a 180-degree turn will move at an angle away from the cow and move toward the

As your horse moves through the turn and accelerates
in direct relation to the speed of the cow, both you and
your horse judge or "read" the speed of the cow and
respond in sync.

back fence. Ideally, the horse should accelerate at approximately the 150- to 170-degree point in the turn.

5. *Accelerate with judgment.*

Your horse accelerates to achieve a controlling position at the cow's neck. As he moves through the turn and accelerates in direct relation to the speed of the cow, both you and your horse judge or "read" the speed of the cow and respond in sync. This acceleration time is crucial to your rhythm with the cow. You do not want to lag behind or "trail" the cow, nor do you want to jump way out beyond the cow. Mirroring the cow's movements translates into beautiful, smooth cutting runs. The presentation looks artistic and flowing rather than mechanical and jerky.

Step #5: *Hold the line/control the cow*

It can be challenging to explain and teach cutting because it is multidimensional. When you work a cow, the situation changes moment to moment. Dozens of variables exist, such as a wild or gentle cow or how aggressive she is in her attempt to return to the herd. Varying situations require different approaches. With that understanding, the essence of cutting is being responsive to an ever-changing scenario. I'm going to outline some simple strategies to help you understand where you should be on a cow to affect the greatest amount of control on her. Use these ideas to present a take-charge, offensive look to the judge.

Holding a line begins at the place where you start working the cow after the cut. Imagine that the place where you drop your hand causes an imaginary line to be drawn across the arena at your horse's hip. The line extends from either side of your horse all the way to the arena walls.

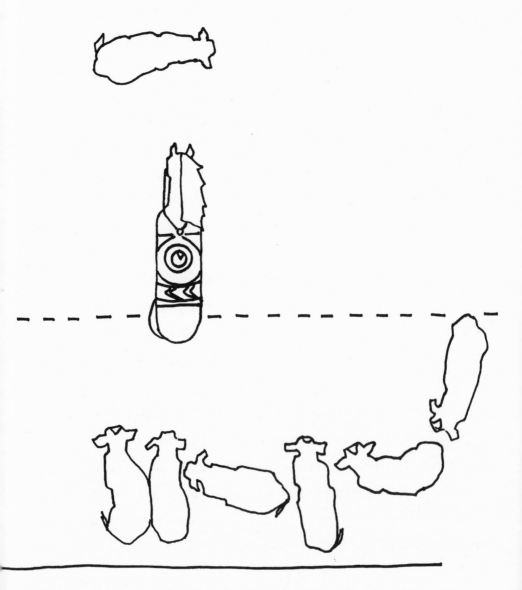

For the discussion here, assume you have cut a cow that can be affected by your moves. You can be an authoritative showman and have the most effect on a cow's behavior by holding your position on an imaginary line as you travel across the arena. Holding a line begins at the place where you start working the cow after the cut. Imagine that the place where you drop your hand causes an imaginary line to be drawn across the arena. The line extends from either side of your horse all the way to the arena walls.

Your goal is to remain on that line as you travel back and forth across the arena with the cow. You do not give ground towards the herd unless the cow puts so much pressure on you that you must, in order to control her position. Often, we find ourselves backing off cattle when there is no reason other than it feels safer. "Staying up" and holding a line is an offensive posture. You maintain pressure on the cow, and you remain intensely involved in the moment. It presents a great, offensive look to the judge which says "I want to show you my horse, I have courage, I'm in the game, and I am confident." Plus, you have the best chance of controlling your cow.

I prefer to control a cow by riding into her at a slight angle towards her neck. Actually, you can stop a cow and turn it anywhere from the neck area forward to the head. But I personally like to focus my eyes on the neck area and then mentally project my center of balance (my lower abdomen and seat) into the neck pocket of the cow. I use my body as something concrete to aim

To "stay up" or "hold the line", focus your eyes on the neck area of the cow, and mentally project your center of balance into the neck of the cow.

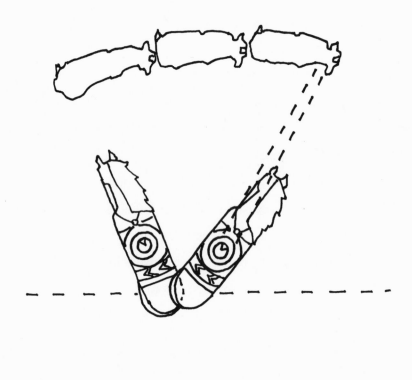

into the cow's neck. When possible, it is always more effective to use your own body to obtain feel rather than using something far outside of yourself, like your horse's head relative to the cow's head. If I try to get my horse's head to be in front of the cow's head, it can feel as if both are dangling beyond me. It becomes difficult to judge where I am. I find that when I ride my horse at an angle into the cow's neck by aiming my own body in that direction (my center of balance), it *naturally* occurs that my horse's head is at just the right distance in front of the cow's head. Keeping things relative to my own body keeps the feeling more anchored instead of feeling abstract. Staying in touch with my center of balance helps me maintain a soft, heavy feel in the saddle. The angle develops easily; the horse's body is in a good position to affect the cow's behavior; and I maintain my center of balance and connection with my horse. Maintaining connection with my horse allows me to feel whether my horse is traveling and stopping on his hindquarters. Again, there is not a right or wrong approach. This is only a personal preference.

Of course, not all cattle have "feel" to them. You may not be able to directly affect their motion. Sometimes cattle move directly away from you instead of towards you, either slightly or dramatically towards the turnback area. When that happens, just shift your riding into a less aggressive mode. Keep your position on your imaginary line across the arena and maintain correctness and rhythm in the turns according to the cow no matter where she

There are basic fundamentals for controlling a cow, including
steps that allow you to control the direction of one cow or a
group as they move away from you.

To get a cow to change its
direction, rein your horse
into the neck or head area of
that cow. This will provide
you with maximum control
of direction.

To get the cow to move away from
you, go toward the hip. Riding to
the hip will give you some control
of movement away from you but
only minimal control of direction.

might be. Because there is not as much intensity when you work a cow that's far away, stay mentally cool, hold your position, and wait for the cow to come back. If you're showing, find a legal place to quit if you've cut a cow that consistently runs away from your horse.

Conversely, when a cow puts intense pressure on your horse to return to the herd, it is imperative to stay focused and aggressively maintain your position into the cow's neck. The distance you retreat from the imaginary line is determined by the pressure the cow is putting on you and your horse. It is easy to feel intimidated and want to back off a tough cow. But that's when your job is to stay tough and maintain your position.

Use Your Body To Help, Not Hinder, Your Horse

In this last half of the chapter, I'll discuss how to use your riding skills to achieve balance, rhythm, and position on a cow. I've dissected your body into parts for the purpose of clear explanations. *Of course, all parts work in harmony to achieve the balance and synchronism of great cutting skills.* When instinct blends with these specific skills, a harmonious ride is created.

There is a physiological transition that occurs immediately after you make your cut and put your hand down. Your seat, upper body, eyes, and legs shift from a "cutting a cow" mode into a "working the cow" mode. Your body assists your horse to achieve correct form, hold a line, and control a cow. What follows are

There is a physiological transition that occurs immediately after you make your cut and put your hand down. Your seat, upper body, eyes, and legs shift from a "cutting a cow" mode into a "working the cow" mode.

guidelines I have found to be generally true for the greatest number of cutting horses and riders. They are offered only as guidelines that can be altered depending upon your horse's training. They are intended to aid your understanding of how your body affects your cutting horse, moment to moment, and are not intended to be inflexible.

The challenge of showing is to achieve and maintain a high level of intensity, action, and control with no visible cues from rider to horse. While the cues may not be obvious or "visible" there's a lot going on with your body that sends loud, clear messages to your horse. Your goal is to send the right signals so you help, not hinder, your horse.

The following section is organized to help you understand how your different body parts affect your riding and your horse and why they are important. Follow the guidelines to achieve correct form, feel, synchronism, and rhythm in your cutting.

1. Seat

The affect on your horse:

Your seat helps the horse:

- ❏ maintain his center of balance,
- ❏ receive a signal from you that a stop is about to occur,
- ❏ stop deeply,
- ❏ maintain his weight on his hindquarters throughout the turn, and
- ❏ maintain his working stability.

To find a deeply centered seat position, round your lower back,
and mentally become aware of your lower abdomen by
concentrating on your breathing. Think of exhaling all the
way through your seat and into your horse's mid-section.

When a rider's seat is not centered, a horse is inconsistent in his movements. He is hindered in his attempts to stop correctly and maintain his center of balance on his hindquarters.

How to find the feel of a centered, soft, anchored seat:

Check to make sure that your seat position in the saddle is correct. Round your lower back, and mentally become aware of your lower abdomen by concentrating on your breathing. Think of exhaling all the way through your seat and into your horse's midsection. When you lose that anchored feeling, do not struggle against your loss of security by forcing your body into the saddle. Instead, bring your awareness back to your abdominal area and center of balance. Exhale and continue. No matter how many times you have to repeat the exercise, you will soon find yourself becoming more and more softly anchored in the saddle.

2. Upper Body

The affect on your horse:

Your upper body helps the horse:

❑ maintain his center of balance throughout the turn and

❑ maintain control and stability in the turn.

If your upper body is leaning forward, backward, or to the side, it is difficult for the horse to maintain his center of balance. The efficiency of his motion will be inhibited.

How to find the feel of a quiet, centered upper body:

Know that leaning is caused by *mentally* being ahead of or

Your upper body helps the horse maintain his center of
balance throughout the turn and maintain control
and stability in the turn.

behind your horse's motion. Instead, relax into the moment. Understand and feel the rhythm of the stops and turns. Coach yourself to be still, let go, and allow your horse to do the work. *Let* him take you with him instead of you trying to *make sure* he's doing his job. Mentally talk to yourself during your ride by using one or several key words like "quiet," "soft," or "still."

3. Eyes

The affect on your horse:

When your eyes are focused on the neck of the cow, it helps your horse maintain his position on the cow consistently and accurately because your concentration is uninterrupted. Some people prefer to look at the heads. Focus wherever you feel most comfortable, but do find a place to focus on the cow and stick with it.

When your eyes drop and look down, your reactions become unpredictable and erratic and your timing is thrown off. Erratic cues to your horse chip away at his confidence and/or correct form.

How to find the feel:

Simply become aware of *softly* focusing on the cow's neck or wherever you prefer. Again, remind yourself with a key word that keeps you focused.

4. Legs

The affect on your horse:

Your legs give your horse information regarding acceleration with the cow and lateral movement up to or away from the cow. These communications occur both while working a cow and while

What the Cow is Doing	What the Rider is Doing	What the Horse is Doing
The cow moves across the arena.	The rider uses his legs/feet to maintain an imaginary line across the arena. Eyes remain focused on the cow's neck.	The horse travels across the arena, balanced on his hindquarters, driving from behind.
The cow begins to slow down.	The rider sinks his hips and center of balance softly down into the horse.	The horse slows motion, using his hindquarters, and mirrors the cow's moves.
The cow stops.	The rider's hips stay deep in the saddle. Lower back is round. Upper body is quiet. Legs are soft and motionless. The rider mentally observes the cow and waits for the next move.	The horse stops deeply in the ground, rocks back, and maintains his center of balance on his hindquarters.
The cow turns.	The rider continues to sit quietly and softly, allowing the turn to be rhythmic. The upper body is motionless. Eyes remain softly on the cow's neck. Legs r emain quiet until the 90-degree point of the turn or after when, if necessary, they are used for direction and/or acceleration throughout the turn.	The horse maintains rhythm and synchronism of the turn by waiting for the cow to move first. Then, the horse pushes off with his front end while rotating on his hindquarters. He accelerates into the cow's neck anywhere between 125 and 160 degrees in the turn.
The cow accelerates.	The rider's eyes continue to tar get the cow's neck ar ea. The rider mentally projects his own body into the cow's neck, feeling the horse remain centered and driving from behind. The rider uses his legs to direct and accelerate, to hold the line, and to maintain a position of control on the cow.	The horse travels across the arena, driving from behind and maintains his position on the line. The horse is ready to stop in the cow's neck.

in the herd.

If you use your legs or feet for balance, or kick your horse inappropriately, it causes him to lose precise control of movement, shift his weight forward, come out towards the cow in his turns, and lose rhythm and confidence.

How to find the feel:

First, find your center of balance. Then, allow your legs to hang ready, but loosely, beneath your hips.

Use your legs at or after the 90-degree point in the turn. Use your legs depending upon your horse's needs. Sometimes you may want to use both legs to accelerate. If necessary, use your herd-side leg briefly when your horse accelerates out of the turn to direct him to the correct angle into the cow. Or, if your horse has not completed the turn or is "coming out," use your cow-side leg to move your horse away from the cow.

Putting it all Together: Balance, Rhythm, Control of the Cow, and Holding the Line

To summarize the above section, on page 186, I have outlined a hypothetical sequence of events involved in working a cow. Follow this sequence to help you and your horse stay balanced, control the cow, and present an offensive look to the judge.

Common Trouble Spots Working a Cow

This section is designed to identify some of the most common

Be Careful With Your Herd-Side Leg

Do not keep it pressed against your horse as you travel across the arena.

Do not use your herd-side leg randomly when it seems as if you should do "*something*" or "*anything*" in a tight situation!

Both of these actions can have serious, negative effects on your horse's performance, such as forcing his attention away from the cow or pushing his rib cage toward the cow. Both instances can put him off balance for the turn and/or signal him to run off.

trouble spots cutters have in riding trained horses. You will understand why it is important to communicate accurately with your
horse, what happens when you don't, and how to use your body to
achieve desired results.

Trouble Spot #1: *Using your herd-side leg randomly in panic*
situations.

The challenge is to stay mentally and emotionally cool when
things seem precarious or vulnerable, i.e., when you are unsure if
your horse will come out of the corner with the cow or if your
horse feels delayed in turning ("hanging"). Stay calm both mentally and physically in those situations. Keep your upper body and
legs quiet or cue your horse as he has been trained.

Why it's important to keep your herd-side leg quiet in panic
situations:

If you give your horse a herd-side kick with your foot at a
vulnerable moment, it will distract him and/or could cause him to
quit. (This excludes horses that were trained to turn in response to
an off-side leg cue. But you still would not want to startle your
horse with a sudden punch!) When you find yourself in a precarious situation, your best bet is to stay physically quiet or use your
cow-side leg judiciously. Keep your eyes on the cow, keep your
body relaxed, and allow your horse to regain his position.

How to find the feel:

Keep your eyes softly focused on the cow at all times. Remain
relaxed, feel the situation, and trust your instincts to either wait or

If you place the horse on the cow off-center, it usually
results in several out-of-sync moves in an attempt to
regain a correct position.

respond appropriately. Stay cool.

Trouble Spot #2: *Releasing your horse off-center of the cow on the cut.*

The challenge is to be pointed at the head and neck area of the cow while making the cut. Remain intently focused on controlling the cow offensively, from the very moment you make your first move on the cow you cut until you put your hand down.

Why it is important to center your horse on the cow:

If your position on a cow is correct, you make a statement to yourself, your horse, the cow, your help, and the judge that you are fully in control of the situation. It is critical to the entire run that your horse start in sync with the cow. If you place the horse on the cow off-center, it usually results in several out of sync moves in an attempt to regain a controlled position. In some situations, a horse will remain off-center the entire time working the cow. If this happens repeatedly, a horse can develop the habit of working a cow off-center.

How to find the feel:

Your upper body and seat are quiet. You arms are free to extend forward to take control of the reins, assertively directing your horse's movements into the cow's neck, and taking charge of the cow on the cut. Your legs are soft but close to the horse's sides so that you can keep the horse's moves directed forward and/or lateral, moment to moment. Your eyes are focused on the neck of the cow. Mentally, you push beyond an imaginary barrier that

"Sit quietly, balanced and loose with still hands. Encourage your horse with your legs as needed."

Helen Groves

transforms your feel from defensive to offensive.

Trouble Spot #3: *Riding too aggressively in the center of the arena and too timidly towards the ends.*

The challenge is to use your legs and feet to help your horse when he needs it and to leave him alone when all is in sync. Usually, in the middle of the arena when the horse and cow are connected, it feels comfortable. There is a natural tendency for inexperienced cutters to feel confident and ride overly aggressive with their feet and legs. When all is going well for horse and rider, it's as if the cutter wants more! At the same time, on the ends, when a horse might need the guidance of your feet and/or legs to get him across the arena, some riders retreat, mentally and physically. It suddenly feels insecure and abstract to be moving at a high rate of speed to the ends. This mental insecurity often translates into physical leg paralysis.

Why it's important to use your legs as needed:

If you don't help your horse maintain his position all the way across the arena, over time he may start to "cheat" on you by falling back away from the cow or by not traveling all the way to the ends. Then, he may try to turn too quickly off the fences or lose cattle on the ends. You can effectively help your horse, when needed toward the ends, and still allow him to express himself when the situation is under control in the center of the arena.

Stay cool in the center of the arena. Use your legs only when necessary to keep your position correct or add some crispness. If

"Always ride your horse to the cow's head and sit down on the corners."

L.H. Wood

you randomly spur because the action feels secure and fun, you might knock your horse out of position and cause everything to get out of sync for the rest of the time you work that particular cow. Whether you are in the center or on the ends, mirror image the cow for a look of total confidence to the judge.

How to find the feel:

Stay patient and focused in the moment. Depending on the situation, use your legs to strategically mirror the cow's moves. Keep your eyes focused on the neck of the cow. If your horse is correct in the middle, stay quiet. Be ready to help your horse with your legs/feet to maintain his position with the cow across the arena.

Trouble Spot #4: *Kicking too soon in the turn.*

The error is using your legs prior to the 90-degree point in the turn. The challenge is to use your legs simultaneously or independently at or after the 90-degree point.

Why it's important not to kick too soon in the turn:

When you kick your horse too soon in the turn, you knock him off balance, distract him mentally, and momentarily lose physical and emotional precision. When you use your legs correctly, you develop precision of motion, control, rhythm, and balance.

How to find the feel:

In order to keep your upper body and seat correctly positioned, think "quiet" and "stay down" (or whatever words are meaningful to you). Exhale during the stop. Sit softly and deeply. Have a

"Let it happen. Don't force it. Take care of the fundamentals."

Winston Hansma

clear understanding of the rhythm and timing of your movements and how to use your legs to meet your horse's unique needs. Keep your eyes focused on the neck of the cow. See your job as being patient and responding to your horse's actual needs as he reaches the acceleration point of the turn.

Now that you have a clear picture of how to work a cow and you understand how your body can affect a trained horse, you are ready to master basic schooling techniques for a trained cutting horse.

This chapter will explain basic schooling techniques

for a trained cutting horse. You will understand

how to execute them, when to apply them, and how

to find feel with your horse. The intent here is

not for you to become a trainer, but to help you

execute basic corrections.

"To me, it is very simple. Go when the cow goes.
Stop when the cow stops. Take one or two steps back
every time you are given the opportunity to keep a
horse on his behind."

Kathy Boone

CHAPTER 7

MAINTAIN YOUR TRAINED HORSE

Everything you do affects your horse and produces a result that
either takes you closer to or further away from your goals. Our
horses need stability and consistency in the communications we
give them. Every horse has strengths and weaknesses. Schooling
is about consistently shoring up your horse's weaknesses and
providing on-going support to insure that his strengths are developed and maintained. If a cutting horse is consistently worked
without being schooled and his weaknesses are left unchecked, he
will develop bad habits. Left uncorrected for a substantial length
of time, those habits can be difficult, if not impossible, to reverse.

"You can make training and showing a cutting horse as simple or as complicated as you want. I've been to both extremes and "simple" has given me the best results. The most important aspects in schooling a horse are the stop and staying in position to control the cow."

Winston Hansma

Basic Schooling Principles

Keep the following points in mind as you read this chapter:

❑ The cow is the catalyst for everything that is done in schooling. Your responsibility is to help your horse maintain precision of motion and rhythm relative to the cow.

❑ In order to build your horse's confidence, he needs consistency.

❑ The use of your hands through a bit or noseband and the use of your legs and/or feet through your calf, heel, and/or spur, should be intended to produce a specific, predetermined response. At the moment that response is achieved, it is your responsibility to release the pressure to let the horse know that he has performed what you intended.

Schooling techniques are about feel. They are more artistic and communicative than scientific. There is no universal approach to schooling, only basic tenants for you to experiment with in various situations.

Schooling Strategy #1: *Keep your horse anchored on his hindquarters.*

The concept: Anchoring a horse is about maintaining the horse's center of balance while working a cow. Your horse should be using his hindquarters throughout the run. You can feel if your horse is anchored when you know you are ready for the next move.

"The basics are the most important foundation on any horse. If a horse has good basics, he is easier to tune. A hard stop and a clean turn are the most important corrections to keep consistent."

Dick Cogdell

For example, you know your horse is ready to stop if, when the cow stops, it feels as if your horse has put on his brakes instead of feeling loose and vague. On an end, you know your horse will stay correct because you can feel him wait and back up a step or two.

Some people might think of staying anchored purely as stopping, but I am referring to a much broader sense of knowing your horse is executing all his moves from his hindquarters.

Why it is important: When a cutting horse works off his rear, he has a foundation for controlled motion. That precision of balance allows him to remain physically controlled, which allows both horse and rider to control the cow.

How to get it: The basic technique to anchor a horse is a two-handed stop (see Chapter Four). You can use it two ways to achieve two different results. First, you can stop and rock your horse back onto his hindquarters to stop forward motion and to prepare for the turn. Second, you can momentarily re-balance your horse; i.e., any time you feel him shift his weight forward you can rock him back on his rear. The latter is only a momentary pause as you rock him back. Then, allow him to "catch up" to the cow. You can also remind your horse to stay collected as he travels or help him stay in position if he gets too far in front of the cow.

Begin with your hands in the regular position for working a cow. Your eyes are focused on the cow's neck or head. As you see the cow slow down or stop, exhale. Then drop your seat as your lower back rounds, signaling to the horse that you want to stop or

When you see the cow preparing for a stop, drop your center of balance softly into your horse. Sometimes your horse will stop, rock back, and collect himself without the aid of your hands. Other times, he may need you to use a two-handed stop to get him to the bottom of his stop prior to turning around.

slow forward motion. Make sure you give your horse time to feel your seat before moving to the next step, a two-handed stop.

To initiate the two-handed stop, slide your left hand (rein hand) up the horse's neck. Take the slack out of the reins by raising your left hand up above the horse's neck. Imagine your arms are on hinges. Do not move your upper body with your arms. Then, your horn-hand grasps both reins simultaneously as it slides down the reins to the horse's neck. This removes all remaining slack out of the reins. Keep your back soft and your seat deep. Steadily bring your right hand down the horse's neck toward your own center of balance as you make contact with the horse's mouth. Smoothly, but firmly, ask the horse to come off of the bit, round his back, and either stop or rock back on his hindquarters.

Five Situations Where You Can Apply
A Two-Handed Stop

Situation #1: *Stop your horse prior to the turn-around.*

In order to achieve this, make sure and watch the cow to instinctively know when she is about to stop. When you see the cow preparing for a stop, drop your seat into your horse softly. Simultaneously, feel if your horse is collecting himself in response to your weight drop in the saddle. Sometimes your horse will stop, rock back, and collect himself without the aid of your hands. Other times, he may not complete the sequence. Instead he might get almost to the bottom of a stop but then come up as he initiates

After getting to the bottom of a stop, some horses
want to turn too quickly instead of waiting for the cow
to move first. Correct this by using several short,
two-handed pulls immediately after the stop to signal
to your horse to wait on the cow to pull him
through the turn.

the turn. Your job is to feel when it is necessary to use a two-handed stop to keep your horse on his hindquarters. You want to be quick and direct with your hand movements, always releasing the bit pressure when the horse gives you the response you seek. Many beginning cutters err by being too timid with their two-handed stop. Be effective—not too easy and not too harsh.

Situation #2: *Remind your horse to wait on the cow.*

After a horse has stopped, he should wait momentarily for the cow to "drag" him through a turn; i.e., the cow stops, the horse stops, the cow moves, the horse moves. After getting to the bottom of a stop, some horses want to turn too quickly instead of waiting for the cow to move first. Correct this by using several short, two-handed pulls immediately after the stop to signal to your horse to wait on the cow to pull him through the turn. This will maintain synchronism and rhythm with the cow.

Situation #3: *Maintain a horse's center of balance throughout the entire turn.*

A horse should keep his weight balanced on his rear throughout the turn. If you feel your horse shift his weight to his front end at any time during the turn, immediately use several short, successive pulls to re-balance him on his rear. Then allow him to complete the turn and accelerate again to regain his position on the cow.

Situation #4: *Maintain correct form and rhythm on the ends.*

Ideally, you want your horse to rock back and allow the cow to

On the ends, your horse should rock back in preparation to move off the wall with the cow, but wait for the cow to make the first move.

The horse waits to come off the fence until the cow gets just past his flank (this is a feel guideline . . . not an absolute).

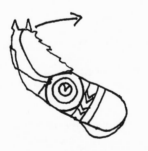

drag him off the fence. The idea here is the same as for situation number two, except it is important to realize that sometimes it feels abstract on the ends. In the center of the arena most people are comfortable and confident, whereas on the ends you can feel like you are in the middle of an open pasture. Horses easily develop the habit of coming off the ends too quickly. When that happens, be alert and ready to keep your horse on his hindquarters by using a two-handed stop and rock him back before he comes off the end. Wait to come off the fence until the cow gets just past the horse's flank (this is a feel guideline, not an absolute). Then, release the pressure and allow him to come through the turn on his own.

If your timing is off and your horse comes off the fence too quickly anyway, you can get back in sync by pausing the horse briefly right after he turns off the fence. Then, allow him to catch up with the cow. It is also a good way to teach a horse how to read what the cow is doing after coming through the turn. These techniques create a smooth rhythm coming off the fence and teach the horse to respond to what the cow is doing and take the appropriate action.

Situation #5: *Teach your horse to travel across the arena using his hindquarters.*

As you move with the cow at any gait, you want to feel ready to stop. This comes from the horse driving his motion from his rear. If you feel your horse shift his weight forward at any time

"Holding a line" also means "staying up and into" the cow when your horse tends to "fall back." At 100-145 degrees through the turn, catch your horse with several short movements with your herd-side leg to keep him from over-rotating.

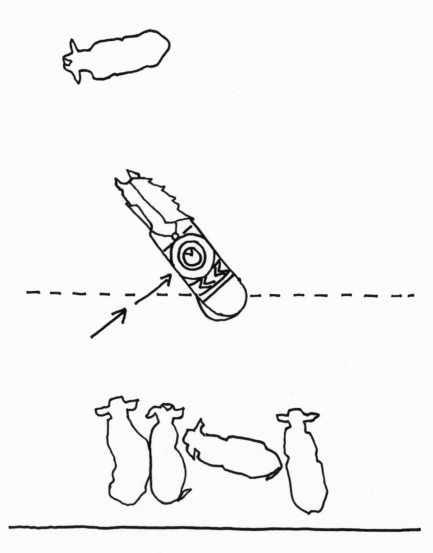

while he's traveling, rock him back using a two-handed stop until he re-balances his weight on his rear. Then, release him and allow him to accelerate again. Repeat this maneuver as often as necessary as you travel across the arena. It is important to keep your horse centered on his rear. If he shifts his weight forward, he loses physical control as well as mental control.

Schooling Strategy #2: *Hold the line*.

The concept: Holding the line is about remaining on an imaginary line across the width of the arena at the point where you were when you dropped your hand after the cut. Maintain that imaginary line position unless the cow pressures you so intently that you must give ground to keep from losing the cow. Holding the line also means maintaining an offensive presence to stop or control a cow (see Chapter Six). It also refers to working on that same imaginary line when the cow drifts away from you.

Why it is important: When your horse maintains correct form and you hold a line across the arena, your performance gains intensity. Holding a line can set you apart from many cutters who are not precise in their response to the cow in terms of depth. It is easy to back off of a cow for no apparent reason. That usually happens when we lack confidence and precision in our riding. Your level of cutting will dramatically improve when you and your horse hold the line and give ground to the cow only when no other option exists.

How to get it: Hold a line by using your legs and/or feet at

Hold a line by using your legs and/or feet at strategic moments during schooling sessions. If you need to use your hands to direct your horse up to the cow, make sure you pair hand and leg cues together.

strategic moments. Sometimes, several short, quick leg and/or foot cues are the most effective. During schooling sessions, you may need to use your hands to direct your horse so that he completely understands your communications. Your hands assure accuracy in your movements. Just make sure you pair hand and leg cues together.

Holding a line also means staying up and into the cow when your horse tends to "fall back." The challenge is to prevent your horse from over-rotating in the turn. There are two different scenarios. The first is most ideal. At 100-145 degrees through the turn, catch your horse with both of your legs or with several short movements with your herd-side leg to keep him from over-rotating. Depending upon your horse's level of training, in practice you may or may not have to use your hands in conjunction with leg and/or foot cues to communicate a clear message of where you want him to go.

This second scenario often happens when you are learning to cut. When you feel that your horse has over-rotated beyond 180 degrees in the turn, you can stop the motion away from the cow by executing a momentary two-handed stop. Then, neck-rein your horse at the appropriate angle toward the cow while simultaneously using your herd-side leg, or both legs.

Another way to think of holding a line is to mirror the cow's movements. Your legs and/or feet are keys to maintain correct position. As you use your legs to accelerate your horse into the

Be Careful With Your Herd-Side Leg

Once you have passed the 180-degree angle and you are heading away from the cow toward the back fence, be careful. If you keep your herd-side leg pressed into your horse to keep him from giving ground, you can create a number of problems. You could cause your horse to travel with his shoulder and/or ribcage extended out toward the cow. This puts the horse at an extreme disadvantage to stop and turn correctly. You could cause your horse to run off due to the constant pressure at his ribcage. Of course, when you show, the use of your herd-side leg may be your only option to regain your position. But instead of keeping constant pressure on your horse's sides, use your legs with quick motions. Be judicious in the use of your herd-side leg.

cow's neck, you will gain a sense of being connected to her. That feeling of connection comes from precision and concentration as you travel across the arena.

Remember that cutting is about making adjustments, moment to moment. If your horse is short, feel his body position as there are several different scenarios to consider. If he is aligned correctly, use both legs to get him into the proper left-to-right position. If he is short and is angled into the cow, use your cow-side leg to move him over and into the correct angle. If he tends to move off the cow towards the herd, use your herd-side leg in quick movements to regain your position up with the cow (prior to the 180-degree point in the turn).

Schooling Strategy #3: *Keep the turn controlled and correct.*

Concept: Keeping your horse balanced and correct throughout the turn.

Why it is important: When your horse shifts his weight forward, brings his shoulder first, or steps forward before the turn is complete, he loses physical accuracy and efficiency in the mechanics of the turn as well as losing the advantage of controlling the cow. A poorly executed turn is also difficult to ride.

How to get it: As you ask your horse to completely stop before making the turn, concentrate and feel the correct alignment of his body. With experience, you will be able to feel if he is balanced and correct or if he is unbalanced through your seat. Even though you are at a slight angle into the cow, the horse's ribcage should be

Keep your horse balanced and correct throughout the turn. As
he rocks back onto his hindquarters and begins to turn, it
should feel as if there is open space on the cow side of the turn
so that the turn can happen easily.

in front of his hips and his shoulder should be squarely in front of his ribcage. As he rocks back onto his hindquarters and begins to turn, it should feel as if there is open space on the cow side of the turn so that the turn can happen easily. If he pushes out with his shoulder and/or ribcage toward the cow in the turn, he either did not stop completely before initiating the turn or, when he stopped, he immediately extended his ribcage and/or shoulder toward the cow.

To correct your horse's alignment, ask him to stop completely and feel whether the horse is collected and if he is in the proper alignment of the hips, ribcage, and shoulders. If you feel your horse lean toward the cow, re-balance him on his hindquarters with the two-handed stop technique as you use your cow-side leg to push his ribcage back underneath his body. When all is set, quickly, but smoothly, release him and allow him to turn. Keep your legs relaxed. *Allow* is the key word here. Do not rush the turn with your legs.

Schooling Strategy #4: *Stay focused.*

Concept: Your horse maintains his intensity with the cow in the middle of the arena or on the ends no matter if the cow is close or far away.

Why it is important: Your horse needs to be ready to move and relate to the cow no matter where he is. Focus and timing are essential to maintaining physical control of your horse as well as control of the cow. Some horses, by instinct, naturally have more

Take Good Care of Your Horse

Many horses stop working at their peak because of joint and/or muscle soreness which may not be easily detected by the naked eye. If a horse is sore and the pain is left unchecked he can develop negative, lifelong associations to cutting that drastically affect performance levels long after a temporary malady has healed. Become committed to taking care of your horse. Learn about your horse's health and soundness. Investigate how to best help him. There are many opinions from a wide variety of perspectives. Research traditional as well as alternative medical treatments and their effectiveness. You alone are responsible for the care, health, and comfort of your horse. Take action before problems become chronic.

cow than others. For the horse that lacks a strong instinctiveness to hunt the cow, it is important that you train him to know that his job is to read the cow, no matter where she is.

How to get it: Get in touch with feeling if your horse is ready to make the next move or not. If he is ready, he will feel rocked back on his hindquarters. As you become aware and experienced, identifying that feel will come easily. If you feel the horse is not intently focused, bring his focus back by using several short, smooth, two-handed pulls. Tuck the horse's nose if necessary. In other instances, you can take him back across the cow by asking for an approximate 160-degree move in the opposite direction of the cow. Then, when the cow moves, he will drag the horse through the turn.

Key Schooling Points

Many common problems cutters face with their horses can be remedied by applying the above universal strategies. But keep the following guidelines in mind for all schooling exercises:

1. The cow is the focus for all movement. Work the cow within a framework of correct form and rhythm while holding a line. Always make corrections in relation to the cow.

2. Use your seat as a focal point to anchor your own center of balance and to feel your horse's balance. Learn to identify whether your horse is working off of his hindquarters or

"Someone once told me to use the KISS method — Keep It Simple Stupid.   I make myself an imaginary line across the arena. I make sure to keep him on his behind whenever the cow stops. Just stop when the cow stops and go when it goes, keep him on his rear, and stay behind the line."

Mitch Farris

not. Always keep yourself and your horse balanced.

3. Keep a clear mental picture of the end result you strive to achieve. Expect positive results. Respond efficiently to the schooling needs of your horse with a "no problem" attitude. Develop your horse's confidence by being instinctive and trusting.

4. Develop flow and rhythm when schooling your horse.

Chronic Problems

Some cutting maladies can be long-term and deeply embedded in your horse's psyche. Quitting a cow, leaking, charging, consistently working a cow off-center, or losing a cow on the wall are examples of problems that developed over time.

If you are experiencing chronic difficulties with your horse, make a plan. If you decide to correct the problems yourself, get a clear idea of how to make the corrections. If you choose to get professional help with your horse, develop a plan with the trainer and give it a certain amount of time. At the end of a predetermined time frame, if the problem has diminished and all is well, carry on. But be aware that some problems are difficult to eradicate. Make a decision about the manageability of your horse's problem. If he is not responding to your personal resources, make a plan which might be to try to find a more suitable horse. Move on to a more positive situation that will reinforce your confidence.

"Practice sharpens, but overschooling blunts the edge. If your horse isn't doing right, the first place to look is yourself. Achievers have self-discipline and are self-critical. Bismark was a great man because he knew when to stop."

Joe Heim

Now that you and your horse are ready, let's move on to winning showmanship, beginning with the herdwork skills outlined in Chapter Eight.

There is no cookbook approach to great

herdwork. But, there are guidelines to help

you feel more in control. This chapter

introduces you to seven basic fundamentals

regarding herdwork.

"Control the situation. Don't let the cows cut you. You cut the cow! As we've heard many, many times, it's better to cut a bad cow good than a good cow bad."

Carole Thorsnes

CHAPTER 8

GAIN CONTROL IN THE HERD

Depending on how challenging you perceive a particular group of cattle to be, it's easy to feel vulnerable and out of control while you are in the herd. At some point, each of us have frozen up in the herd and merely hoped everything would work out. But, when you understand some basic dynamics of herdwork, you'll gain a wonderful sense of control.

In essence, you'll approach the herd as if you are its manager—in charge of making a plan, setting out to execute it, and then responding to a three-dimensional, ever-changing scenario. Herdwork is a dynamic process. No two situations and no two

During your cut, it is desirable to have cattle loosely grouped in a fan shape so you can view individual cattle more easily.

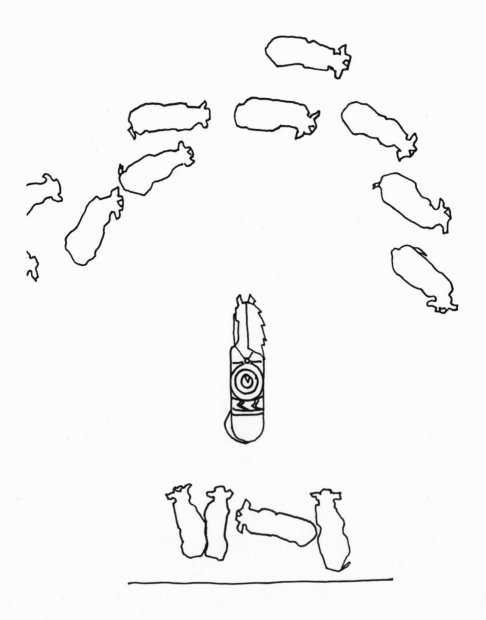

cattle you encounter will be the same. Your job is to simply execute fundamental herdwork skills. Only then will you gain a
sense of confidence and maximize your horse's show potential.

As you experiment with the techniques in this chapter, you'll
soon begin to trust your feel and instinct. You'll become flexible
and responsive to changing situations. You'll be like a symphony
conductor, orchestrating gorgeous cuts with authority and presence
in the middle of the arena. You'll maintain your cool and keep the
calm demeanor necessary to execute make-it-or-break-it decisions.

The Ideal Cut

Let's begin with a vision of the ideal cut. Once you have this
picture in your mind, I'll describe the steps that lead you there.
My description starts from near the finish of the cut and works
backwards.

The most important goal is to cut clean, in the middle of the
arena. In order to best accomplish this, you want to end up with
cattle driven up to the center of the arena forming a loose, fan
shape in front of your horse. Ideally, they should be 15 to 20 or
more feet beyond the rest of the herd on the back fence. When
cattle are loosely grouped or spread out in a fan shape, you can
view individual cattle better. You can make better decisions about
their behavior based on what you see. It also helps cattle stay
more responsive to the horse because they are not in a tight wad,
and they are in a position to see the horse. In this situation, you

When a horse enters the herd at the back fence, cattle at the rear
see the horse, and then move forward. As they push toward the
center of the arena, they bump into cattle in front of them,
surprising those cattle as they press forward. As that group moves,
they bump into unsuspecting cattle in the very front. The whole
group becomes more and more compressed as it inches forward.
Then, the cattle become anxious and tend to spin off in layers. As
each layer spins off, the next inner layer of cattle are surprised. The
last remaining cow may or may not be a desirable one.

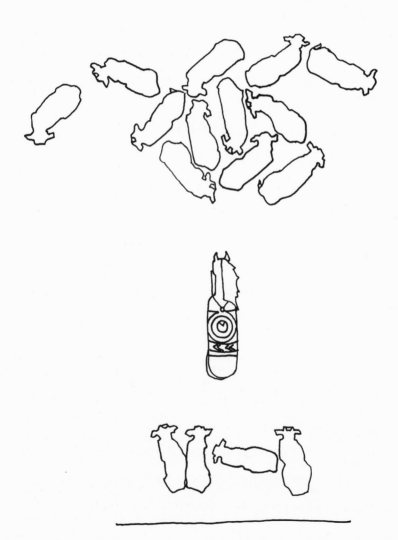

and your horse have a better chance of connecting to cattle in a smooth, effortless way.

What you do not want is for the cattle to be driven out so that they form a tight, milling, anxious group in front of your horse. When that happens, you can't read how individual cattle will act because they are moving in mass and in circles and don't show their individuality.

As cattle drift back to the herd during the cut, your job is to observe, moment to moment, and respond appropriately to cut the best cow for that particular situation. You then take charge of the cow you choose in the middle of the arena by stepping confidently to her head and neck area. Make sure you pause your horse's forward motion. Smoothly lower your hand and begin working.

The most effective cattle selection strategy is a combination of cutting specific cattle and cutting for shape. At this point in our discussion, I believe it's important to define cutting for shape and cutting specific cattle. Cutting for shape is the process of driving a group of cattle out to the center of the arena and cutting whichever cow best presents itself on that cut. You do not have specific cattle in mind. During shape cuts, you use your eyes to scan the group of cattle in front of you as you patiently wait to make your decision about which cow to cut.

Cutting specific cattle is the process of entering the herd with the intent to cut pre-selected cattle. Cutting specific cattle involves watching them as they are settled and/or worked by other

As cattle drift back to the herd during the cut, your job is to observe, moment to moment, and respond appropriately to cut the best cow for that particular situation.

Then take charge of the cow you choose in the middle of the arena by stepping confidently to her head and neck area. Make sure you pause your horse's forward motion. Smoothly lower your hand and begin working.

cutters in order to select the best cattle based upon your observa-
tions. You switch to a shape cut if your pre-selected cattle can't be
cut smoothly in the center of the arena. Many experienced cutters
enter the herd with three or four good cattle in mind. As they walk
through the herd, they manipulate it through movements and turns,
placing good cattle in prime cutting positions. If a cutter's game
plan begins to go awry—because of the ever-changing dynamics of
the cattle, helpers, or their own moves—their finely-tuned instincts
allow them to be very flexible and cut the best cow for the situation—always in the center of the arena.

With that picture planted in your mind, this chapter will talk
you through seven steps during your cut. Follow me now and
begin to see your herdwork skills as a step-by-step process.

Step #1: *Preparing to Enter the Herd*

In the moments before you walk to the herd, it's important to
complete a pre-run ritual. A ritual is very personalized and is used
to focus your mind on your job and ground yourself in positive
emotions. Some examples might include backing your horse a few
steps, taking several deep breaths, or pulling your hat down. You
might also have a specific series of phrases you say to yourself
such as "shoulders back" or "chin up" or "stay cool." It doesn't
matter what the ritual is. It just matters that you do it consistently,
no matter what else is going on around you. Your ritual will get
you mentally prepared. And, because the things you do in those
moments will signal to your horse that it is time to work, your

Before you walk to the herd, complete a pre-run ritual.

Both you and your horse will feel focused and ready.

Just after your ritual—or as a part of it—look at the herd, think about your job for that group of cattle.

Now, as you walk to the herd, either review your plan about the cattle and/or remind yourself to "stay cool" or "step up" on the cut.

horse will benefit from your ritual as well.

Step #2: *Walking Toward the Herd*

As you walk to the herd, maintain control of your eyes. Your eyes play a critical role in controlling your mind. When your eyes dart around, your mind follows. The key is to choreograph your eyes for all aspects of your run. Just after your ritual—or as a part of it—look at the herd, think about your job for that group of cattle. Earlier, as you watched the cattle being settled, you may have studied how they acted and made a plan. You then decided to cut for shape, cut specific cattle, or both. Now, as you walk to the herd, either review your plan about the cattle and/or remind yourself to "stay cool" or "step up" on the cut. Then, if anything in particular about the herd comes up as you approach the herd—the cattle you choose seem too wild or too numb—stay cool.

Trust that you'll be able to make good decisions. No matter if things are happening as planned or not, you can still give yourself strategic reminders. For example, if the cattle look numb, remind yourself to be aggressive. If they are wild, remind yourself to watch and move efficiently. In summary, between the time you complete your ritual and the time you walk to the herd, review your plan and, if necessary, revise it—all the while maintaining control of your eyes and your posture as you walk toward the herd.

Step #3: *Entering the Herd*

The next step is entering the herd. Some cutters enter the herd randomly, make a turn in the herd, walk forward, stop, and then

Enter the herd at an angle near the top or side of the group to
get the cattle moving forward to the center of the arena.

wait for the cow who happens to be the last one. They don't have a plan. But how and where you enter the herd has a definite effect on cattle and on how your entire cut evolves. The goal is to enter the herd quietly and strategically to get the cattle moving forward smoothly. This gives your cut the appearance of being controlled, calm, and offensive. If you ride in haphazardly, either pushing too hard or not driving out enough, the cut will look random and vulnerable. Making cuts, just like working a cow, is rhythmic. There's a flow, an awareness, and a responsiveness.

For most cuts (except for "peeling" a cow), cattle walk toward the center of the arena in a group. How they walk out, away from the herd, is important. Ideally, you want cattle to file loosely to the center of the arena instead of winding up wadded together in a tight group.

To accomplish this, I like to enter the herd near the front or the side. I call it "slicing" the herd. This causes a disturbance in the cattle near the point of entry. This, in turn, causes the cattle near the area of the disturbance and their "friends" to move away from you and your horse. When you enter from the front or side of the herd, the cattle that first begin to move toward the center become the "lead" cows. The others near the lead cattle usually follow them as they make their way to the center of the arena. With this approach, depending upon how fresh or how much they've been used, the group will arrive there in a loosely-formed group because they moved behind the lead cows.

"Cut a cow in the middle of the arena that is looking at you."

Jack Newton

I prefer to use this slicing method to move cattle to the center of the arena instead of entering the herd near the back fence and driving out from there. When you drive out from the back, the front cattle move out involuntarily because they've been pushed from behind. This tends to form a tightly knit group of cattle moving in unison. As you continue to drive forward, you may (depending on how wild the cattle are) wind up with a group of surprised, anxious cattle that are spinning and swirling. They are unaware of the horse and tend to overreact in their movements. It can be like a hornet's nest. The cattle swarm and roll in very unpredictable ways.

Step #4: *Making the Turn*

After you've entered the herd and got the cattle moving forward as easily as possible, the next step is making the turn. This step is key to the success of your cut because as you make the turn, where you step (straight ahead, or angled left or right) has everything to do with guiding how and where the cattle move.

The goal is to get a group of cattle 15 to 20 or more feet away from the herd to the center of the arena. Fresher cattle will be more willing to step towards the center. But the more used they are and the more they understand the game, the more quickly they will turn and attempt to head back to the back fence. So, your job, as you make the turn, is to quickly identify where the flow of cattle is heading by observing where the lead cattle are going. If necessary, move your horse to the place that best moves the cattle to the

As you make your move to control the direction of the flow of cattle, you also determine how much push or aggressiveness is needed to get them moving at a consistent, smooth pace. Drive out to set up your cut in the middle of the arena.

center of the arena. Depending on what direction you seek, you'll angle your horse left or right or move with them from behind.

As you make your move to control the direction of the flow of cattle, you also determine how much push or aggressiveness is needed to get them moving at a consistent, smooth pace. Every time you make the turn, you create a natural momentum of cattle movement forward. It is essential that you take advantage of that momentum and keep it going in a smooth, continuous motion. Once the cattle stop that natural movement and you try to start the flow forward by getting them moving again, it's like trying to swim upstream.

Many cutters make the mistake of making the turn and stopping out of habit instead of responding to and moving with the cattle during those critical seconds. After all, the idea has been drilled into you to stay quiet in the herd. But, when you stop only for the sake of stopping, often the cattle you seek to drive out will stop their forward motion. Too often, they are not far enough out from the rest of the herd. Your job is to find the natural rhythm and momentum within every herd and take advantage of it as you drive out to set up your cut in the middle of the arena.

Step #5: *Making Good, Spontaneous, Moment-to-Moment Decisions During the Cut*

Cutting for Shape

Now that you've driven a group of cattle up to the center of the pen for the cut, you'll face the moment of truth that will determine

Cutting for shape has everything to do with calm, cool, and
spontaneous judgment. Stay in a search-and-find mode,
looking for the cattle furthest away from you at the top of
the group and moving to the center of the arena.

if your cut is clean, pretty, smooth, and centered or erratic and rough. The first step is becoming very skilled at cutting for shape, which involves learning how to scan and search the herd to select the best cow for that cut. This skill must be developed well before a cutter can advance to cutting specific cattle. Cutting for shape involves so much more than simply standing out in front of the herd and waiting for the last cow. After all, the last cow might be the same bad cow that has been out front and in the way every time or the one that has run over the last three cutters. Cutting for shape has everything to do with calm, cool, and spontaneous judgment. Although the first step for beginning cutters is to use their eyes and simply wait to see how the situation unfolds, soon it will be time to improve. The real advancement in shape cutting comes as you begin to recognize and feel the flow of the herd, think clearly, and make great decisions easily on the spot—helping you avoid bad cattle.

A word of caution: for beginning cutters who are just learning to cut for shape, it is natural to go with the first cow that moves. Emotions run high and anxiety abounds, which makes brain-wave patterns erratic. It can feel like you are moving on the inside at 100 miles per hour. Your vision gets narrow as varying degrees of panic set in. In this state, it is a totally natural impulse to go with a cow that moves away from the group quickly.

Instead, stay cool and train your eyes to observe the cattle near the end of and on the outside of the flow. Stay in a search-and-find

Once you have become comfortable with cutting for shape, the next step is making your cuts to facilitate cutting specific cattle.

The key to this skill is entering the herd, making the turn, and stepping out with the intent of smoothly arranging the cow or cattle you want to cut to be on the outside and end of the flow of cattle.

Put your horse on the cow you cut, with authority.

mode looking for the cattle furthest away from you at the top of the group and moving to the center of the arena. At the same time, be watching for a cow that appears calm—head level, eyes soft, body relaxed.

Cutting Specific Cattle

Once you have become comfortable with cutting for shape, the next step is making your cuts to facilitate cutting specific cattle. The key to this skill is entering the herd, making the turn, and stepping out with the intent of smoothly arranging the cow (or cattle) you want to cut to be on the outside and end of the flow of cattle.

An important skill of cutting specific cattle is the art of observing cattle, moment to moment, in order to perceive details of how your pre-determined cow (or cattle) is acting. You then identify whether or not your particular cow wants to be cut as it moves through the herd. For example, you have tentatively identified a yellow, horned cow as the one you want and you are moving through the herd so she will end up on the outside of the flow. You also notice which other cattle are with her. But you notice out of the corner of your eye that she is acting very nervous as the other cattle walk by her and she has her head elevated. In an instant, as your mind processes that information, you switch gears and your eyes immediately search for another cow in a good position to be cut. With your eyes in a search mode, you switch to a shape cut and run through a mental checklist: What's out here? Which cow

Driving Out

When you drive out in a continuous, fluid motion you help your horse as well as your cut. Cutting horse training consistently reminds a horse to do everything on its hindquarters while working a cow. If you make your cut too close to the herd, you may have to start your run by kicking your horse forward in order to get him up to the cow. This takes him off his rear end and starts him on his front end, the very opposite of what years of training has taught him. If this kind of cut is repeated consistently in shows, some horses associate showing with working on their front end. Instead, be smooth. Step up away from the herd to make your cut. Then you will be set up at the best place to make the cut, and your horse will begin working on his hindquarters.

The key to driving out is to use your eyes. Even as you walk into the herd, immediately begin looking to see where and in what direction the flow is going. Then, if necessary, after you make your turn towards the center of the arena, move toward the heads and necks of the group's lead cattle. This will guide the entire herd in a forward direction.

When you drive out, it will also allow you to work any type of cow in the best manner. Obviously, a good cow works great in the middle of the arena. But if a cow you have cut turns out to be bad, you may be able to survive and quit quickly if she is further away from the rest of the herd.

All of these actions result in an offensive, take-charge cut and you've started your horse in the middle of the arena.

is the best for this situation? A wide field of vision and your ability to scan and see what's really happening are the keys to this instinctive skill.

If you are inexperienced at cutting specific cattle, you can become discouraged with this skill in the beginning when it does not result in successful cuts. But it is not the idea of cutting specific cattle that is the problem. Instead, it may be a lack of flexibility and spontaneity. If you are only focused on cutting a pre-selected cow, you may not be responsive to what is actually going on around you as you ride through the herd. Observe the entire situation. Constantly gather information to support or negate your theory that cows A, B, or C are good candidates.

When you first experiment with cutting specific cattle, be patient. It will take time to master this skill. Practice by watching cattle on other cutters' cuts. Watch the cattle you have chosen as well as others as another cutter rides through the herd. Observe the flow. See exactly what is going on in the big picture—not just in front of the cutter. This technique will develop your eyes and help you make important decisions about the cut, moment to moment. Then, apply the same approach to your own herdwork.

Step #6: Putting Your Horse on the Cow With Authority

You've been cool. You've read the situation as it unfolded on the cut. Now it's time to step up and take charge of the cow you're cutting. Make a bold statement to the judge and put your horse on the cow with authority. It says that you are confident and there to

Communication With Helpers
is Essential

Two common errors made in regards to stepping out for
the cut are not having a plan for cutting shape or specific
cattle and not discussing that plan with your helpers.
Many inexperienced cutters enter the herd and are
coached by their helpers to "wait, wait, wait" because
their helpers assume the cutter is walking out blindly.
Develop a plan and discuss it with your helpers. Include a
discussion of stepping out strategically and smoothly
to the middle of the arena.

show your horse. You also say to the horse, "This is the cow we are going to cut." And it makes the cow aware that you are taking charge of her. But most of all, when you step into the neck of the cow with authority, it causes you to start your work on that cow offensively. Just make sure that after you step to control the cow, you pause your horse's forward motion so that he can begin working from a stopped, rocked-back position on his hindquarters.

On the cut, I like to step into the neck as a target area for controlling the direction of a cow. Sometimes aiming at the cow's head can be vague. Technically, you could be one to five or more feet in front of the cow and still be at her head. But when you step into the cow's neck, you focus your attention on one specific area of the cow.

If the cow you cut begins moving very quickly toward the herd, you may legally keep your hand up while the cow is moving until the rest of the cattle pass beyond your horse's hip. Judge their position by using your peripheral vision to see where they are. Then, smoothly but quickly lower your hand to avoid a one-point reining penalty. Once you put your hand down, your whole body position changes. Your back rounds and your legs soften as you sink deep into the horse's center of gravity and let the horse work.

Step #7:   Developing *Feel* with Experience

Whether you cut for shape and/or cut specific cattle, there is a feel in the herd that dictates how you proceed from where you enter until the cut is complete. *Feel* is your response to the energy

Enter the Herd from the Middle

If you're cutting cattle that are sour, hard to drive, and compressed on the back fence, I suggest you use a technique I learned from Bill Freeman. A great way to enter a difficult herd is from the middle. This causes two lines of cattle on either side of the cutter to move forward toward the center of the arena. It is essential that herd holders be involved in this plan as they help form a chute of blocked escape on each side of the cutter. In this plan, the cattle advance to the center of the arena from the front of the herd instead of from the back.

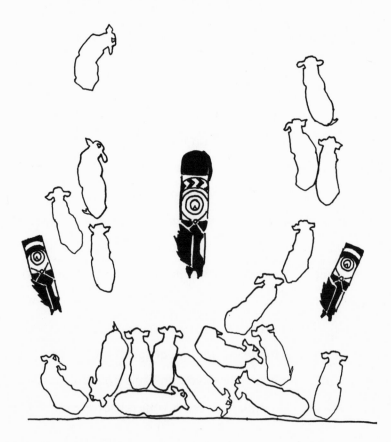

of a particular herd of cattle combined with how your plan unfolds. *Feel* determines how you move through the herd as cattle respond to you. In an instant, you will begin to process what is going on within a herd. When and where are you aggressive? When and where are you quiet and waiting? As you develop feel, you become instinctive. It is a combination of being calm, aggressive, confident, and bold all at once in response to whatever herd you are in. Developing feel will allow you to automatically complete the previous six steps in this chapter.

Here are some key pointers. From the time you cause that first ripple of motion as you enter the herd, be aware that the moves you and your horse make will affect the cattle. Then, the response of the cattle will direct you. For example, as you press forward, the cattle move. As you back off, the cattle stop or at least slow their pace. You angle left, the cattle move right. It's a combination of making a move, observing the cattle, and then momentarily backing off to observe the response of the cattle. Then, move strategically again. Cow response. Observe. Move. Cow response. Observe. Move.

As you practice and experience this give-and-take interaction, your instincts will take over. Give yourself time. Always keep your vision soft and scanning. Breathe. As you begin to feel as though you're responding to and managing the herd, cutting will become more fun instead of intimidating.

In horrible cattle, the actions you take in the herd are still the

Stay Tuned-in to Your Horse on the Cut

It is easy to become so involved with the mechanics of making the cut that you become unaware of how your horse is feeling underneath you. From the time you enter the herd, it should be your goal to keep your horse clearly aimed in the direction you desire to go. Become aware how your horse feels as you drive out for the cut. If he feels inattentive you can gently stop him, rock him back, then give him a nudge with your feet to continue forward. If he begins to go sideways, use your legs as well as your hands to immediately straighten his direction. All the while, show absolutely no negative emotion on the outside. Make sure that you—not your horse— orchestrate the most effective moves to begin working the cow properly.

same. They just evolve at a faster pace. The feel is still there; it just requires more confidence and efficiency. It's up to you to stay calm and focused, and plan how you will handle a tough group of cattle. I suggest you experiment with the tip on page 248.

Once you've mastered the mechanical skills of herdwork, listening to and trusting your instincts will allow you to make the highest percentage of good decisions.

Now that you've learned some fundamentals of great herdwork skills, you're ready to begin studying cattle.

This chapter is designed to help you weave

cattle selection into your overall cutting plan.

"Studying cattle becomes more important the deeper into the herd I draw. Knowledge of the cattle that have been worked gives me a quiet confidence."

James Hooper

CHAPTER 9

STUDY CATTLE

A high-marking, competitive cutting run begins with a beautiful cut. It appears effortless and flows with poise, style, and authority. Although it sometimes appears as if that magical cow just happened to be there, for most experienced cutters, it was the result of studying cattle.

No matter how skilled you become at studying cattle, your predictions will never be 100 percent accurate. The process is intangible and elusive. Your goals should be to learn to identify cattle physically as well as to predict their behavior when separated from the group. Over time, you will increase the percentage

"Some people say there is no way to know what a cow is going to do until you cut her. That's true; but by studying the cattle, it improves your odds, and you need every edge you can get."

Dick Cogdell

of times you are correct in your predictions. When you begin to know the good cows from the bad with a high degree of accuracy, the results can be very exciting. Your approach to cattle will shift from fearful and vulnerable to strategic. You will see picking cattle as a fun, high-level skill.

The purpose of this chapter is to help you weave cattle selection into your overall cutting plan. The highest level herdwork plan includes knowledge and selection of cattle combined with flexibility and cutting for shape if your chosen cattle cannot be cut. Your number one goal is to cut cleanly in the center of the pen. Use the herdwork skills discussed in Chapter Eight to maneuver your favorite cattle to the center of the arena. But, if that doesn't work, shift to the best cow for the situation. The wisdom of "a bad cow cut well is better than a good cow cut badly" is timeless.

The art of watching cattle can be divided into two parts: describing cattle physically and predicting their behavior.

DESCRIBING CATTLE PHYSICALLY

Your goal is to be able to tell one cow from another relative to the cattle in that particular group. For example, what matters is that you are able to differentiate between most, if not all, of the 10 black cattle, the 12 red cattle, the six yellow cattle, and the two brindles in your bunch. You want to feel that you can recognize your cattle instantly and make confident, split-second decisions in the herd.

"Always study
your own cattle.
Never expect
someone else
to study them
for you."

Millie Kay Bouget

Differentiating cattle is most successfully accomplished by watching them as they enter the arena, throughout the settling process, and while other cutters are working prior to your turn.

General Overview

Get an overview of the cattle when they first enter the arena and mentally note your impressions. Determine their overall colors. Are they heavy? Do they look healthy or sick? Are they good quality cattle?

After the overview is complete, start noting specifics either in your head or with pen and paper. Some cutters get down to the nitty-gritty of watching cattle with a notepad. Others don't. What matters is keeping cattle clearly identified with vivid descriptions. For me, written notations provide an instant reference. It gives me confidence that I can remember all my prospects.

Color/Breed

I sort cattle first by determining the predominant colors and/or breeds. There are basic colors of cattle—black, red, white, yellow, brown, brindle, roan, and gray—and many variations in between. By breaking the cattle into color groups, they become instantly easy to identify. Then you can break them into sub-categories of color and/or breed. For example, if half the herd is red, your mind can automatically switch gears again and begin to sort within the red group; i.e., dark reds, solid reds, light reds, motley face, red

You can differentiate cattle by noting head characteristics.

This cow's head could be described as "peaky poll" with a bonnet and a streak.

This is a left blinder, right tear drop, muley (no horns).

This is a "two-dot mott."

necks, Santa Gertrudis, Limousin, and Herefords.

Color perception can be different from one person to another, so it is important that your helpers know exactly what you are talking about when you describe a cow. You can make the process fun by calling cattle funny or unique names like "Snow White" or "woolly bear." It helps to use semantic markers, because they are less likely to be forgotten.

If a herd is predominantly one color, then I know I have to work harder. But the more practice you have studying cattle, the more you will automatically begin to spot subtle cattle features and see that they don't really all look alike. Each cow is unique.

Once you have sorted the herd by color, it is time to move on to less obvious characteristics.

Head Descriptions

Another way to differentiate cattle is by looking at their heads. There are a few key hallmarks that will allow easy and quick identification: head shape, patterns of color in the face, the presence or absence of horns, and the eyes.

An unusually shaped head can allow you to quickly identify a cow. You can assign a descriptive name like "cone head" or "peaky poll." Since there is no official language recognized by the cutting industry for describing cattle, it's important you make sure your helpers understand your characterizations.

The term "motley" is a description for unusual patterns and/or

Another way to sort cattle is by looking at the shape of their horns.

"Spike"

"Flattop"

"Devil"

colors in a cow's face. If there are several motley-faced cattle in the herd, they can be distinguished by recognizing shapes, designs, or patterns. A bridge-nose mott is a cow that has a band of color on its nose that could be either wide or narrow and may or may not slope up toward the eyes. If the color does not go all the way across the nose, that cow might be called a partial bridge-nose.

If the cow has only one spot of color on its face, for example, you could call it "one spot" or "bullet hole." Two spots of color might be called "two spot" and so on.

Sometimes the coloring on a cow's face may resemble a unique shape that can be quickly identified. For example finding a "heart-mott" or "lightening-mott" in the bunch is a lot easier than trying to analytically describe such a pattern.

Horns

Another way to sort cattle is by looking at the tops of their heads to determine whether or not they have horns. Then, the next step in differentiating between cattle is to look at the shape of their horns. For example, a cow whose horns curve inwards toward one another might be called "devil horn." The cow with the small, cleat-like horns might be called "spike horn." "Roll-top" could be the cow with or without horns that looks like she has a long cylinder growing across the top of her head.

Note various differences among cattle, pay special attention to brands, identifying marks, ear tags, and manure or dirt patterns on specific cattle. For example, although the entire herd may be marked with the same brand, it can be helpful to look for differences in how those brands appear.

This cow has a large manure stain below and to the right of the brand.

This cow has a high tail set with "tail feathers" down the tail.

Haircoat

If there are still discrepancies in identifying one red, horned cow from another, look at the cow's haircoat. Although a group of cattle may be colored similarly, the type and texture of each cow's haircoat might be obviously different. Although hair color may be solid on a cow, upon closer inspection you may see that there are actually two slightly different colors, one on their neck, the other on the rest of their body. One cow's haircoat may be smooth and slick while the other one is fuzzy, fluffy, or very dull. Immediately, you can tell those cattle apart.

Brands, Ear Tags, and Other Markers

As you note various differences among cattle, pay special attention to brands, identifying marks, ear tags, and manure or dirt patterns on specific cattle. For example, although the entire herd may be marked with the same brand, it can be helpful to look for differences in how those brands appear. Note specifics, such as peeling, raw marks, uneven marking, and even incomplete brands that have hair growing where it shouldn't be. For example, the yellow cow with the manure stain on her left hip that looks like a rectangle will be easy to pick out from the 20 other yellow cattle once you have identified that marker.

The more you need to distinguish between cattle, the more you rely on subtle descriptors. Identifying cattle is not a science. There is no official language nor are there any official terms that must be

This paint cow has a half white tail which could be easily spotted from your horse.

This heifer might have an exceptionally wooly hair coat as compared to others in a herd of cattle.

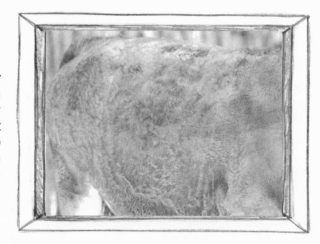

used to describe cattle. If you have a way that works for you, go for it. Just be sure that you communicate with your helpers.

PREDICTING BEHAVIOR

As you physically differentiate cattle, notice their behavior. A great way for you to become more adept at judging cattle is to study them in classes other than your own. By watching cattle in other classes and trying to accurately predict their behavior, you accomplish two things.

First, you gain more experience. Second, by picking out cattle when you don't feel pressure, you can relax, practice, and be bolder in your predictions.

Watch and study high-level competitors. Study cattle and make your choices by picking out desirable behaviors. Then, pretend you are the next cutter to work for each person in that group. Watch the cattle you picked as they are worked and see how they behave. Also, notice the choices made by those high-level competitors you watch. The best way to practice studying cattle is in no-pressure situations.

It is important to look for cattle that show interest in and respond to the horse. Begin your study while the herd is being settled. Pay particular attention to how the cattle act around the settler's horse. Any movements made by a potential cow should be smooth and consistent. As the settler approaches the cow, an ideal response is for her to turn into the pressure and then move

"If you don't feel comfortable picking a really good cow, just watch the cattle to see which ones you know you want to stay away from."

Mitch Farris

away with ease while continuing to look at the horse. If she increases her pace, it should only be slightly. Often, the moment pressure is removed from a good cow, she will stop or resume her original pace. If a cow is numb and doesn't move away from the horse, it should be placed on your list of undesirables.

The settler's job is to calm the cattle, get them used to horses and their new surroundings, and introduce them to the back fence. The settler allows them to move to the center of the arena and then to the back fence several times. This is an important time for you to watch the herd to see how they act and move.

A good cow will move smoothly away from the settler's horse and may even stop, turn, and look back at the horse. A curious cow may even walk up to the horse's head or rear. When the settler's horse approaches the head or neck of a good cow, she should easily stop. After she stops, she might change her direction of travel or continue on with relaxed ease. These are very desirable characteristics.

On the other hand, cattle that appear openly nervous or tense, who wheel in the opposite direction of the settler's horse, lower their heads and burrow to the back of the herd, or dart erratically in and out of the herd, are undesirable.

Cows, like people, have a "bubble" which is an imaginary space in which a person or horse may trespass before that cow feels "invaded" and moves. People call it "invading my space" or "on my turf." It is that magic, invisible area that surrounds us and

"Keep track of what has been cut. Remember what has been lost. Remember some that were good but not used much."

Helen Groves

is the zone in which we feel most comfortable. When someone steps within our comfort zone, we feel crowded and feel the urge to step back or move away. The same is true for cattle. Some wilder cows have a large bubble and even the slightest movement in that cow's direction will cause her to retreat. More gentle cattle have a small bubble where you have to be closer to the cow before she starts to move. Determining how far into a cow's bubble you can trespass is important in predicting how she will act alone in the center of the arena when you cut her. The best cattle have a medium bubble.

Studying cattle and learning how to predict their behavior is a learning process that is never complete. No matter how much practice you have and no matter how comfortable you are in identifying and sorting cattle into groups, no two cows are the same. And just because that tiger-striped cow ran over you last weekend doesn't mean that another similar looking cow in front of you today is going to do the same. Cattle are unpredictable and no matter how skilled you become, you will never be 100 percent correct. But with practice comes experience and with experience comes priceless knowledge. If you earn your experience sitting in the bleachers at a weekend cutting or sitting in the coliseum seats at the NCHA Futurity pretending you are your favorite top-level cutter, it doesn't matter. The time and effort you put into that practice will make all the difference in actual cutting situations.

I realized that if I worked hard and got good at watching cattle

"Studying cattle gives you a game plan even if you cut shape. You know cattle that are bad and the potentiall good ones."

Ronnie Nettles

I could draw up anywhere in a group of cattle and feel comfortable. In fact, you will become more and more comfortable with later draws as you use the time to differentiate cattle. By expending time studying cattle and predicting their behavior, you will impact every other area of your cutting experience. The confidence boost that comes with accurately picking cattle will make you approach all you do with more authority. Although you never know exactly what a cow will do until you cut it, when you invest time honing your cow watching skills, you stack the deck in your favor.

Now you're ready for polish on your personal showmanship style.

This chapter is divided into three primary sections.

The first discusses preparation strategies performed

prior to the day of the show. The second section

reviews preparation ideas for the day of the show

prior to your run. And the third section discusses

outstanding presentation skills for your run.

"Remember, luck is when preparation meets opportunity. Be patient, let it happen, don't try to force it. Have your horse ready, tell yourself you've done the best job possible preparing him (and believe it) and go cut the best cows left down there."

Winston Hansma

CHAPTER 10 _____

DEVELOP YOUR OWN SHOWMANSHIP STYLE

Your job in the show arena is to present your best and your horse's best with authority. Horses, like people, have strengths and weaknesses. Even the all-time best horses have things to improve. The challenge is to expose your horse's unique talents and skills and to demonstrate that uniqueness with an air of supreme confidence.

It's no accident that some riders show different horses with varying talents and capabilities and still routinely make it to the finals and winner's circle. Those riders possess excellent presentation skills. They use those skills each and every time they show,

"Have a plan. Execute it."

Kathy Boone

no matter the horse. When you watch them ride, they look like they want to be there. They have a cool, calm exterior and you can bet that their mind is totally focused on the job at hand.

Preparation Prior to Show Day

I can't over-emphasize the importance of preparation. It builds confidence . . . and confidence is the emotion of successful competitors. The process of being ready has two parts—one is preparing yourself and the other is preparing your horse.

Prepare Yourself

The mental and emotional preparation necessary for competition involves the skills and exercises in Chapter Five. I re-emphasize here that the mental and emotional aspects of cutting are skills, not talents. Mental preparation has a powerful impact on your expression of technical skills because when you are calm, focused, and confident, your body is free to perform well. If you don't practice being calm and focused prior to show day, you will have difficulty staying cool and being consistent in a show situation.

The technical aspects of preparation are individual. You don't have the same physical capabilities as your friend or your trainer— you have your own strengths and weaknesses. It's important to ask and answer the following question. What foundation skills do I need to improve; i.e., balance, getting out of the herd, position on the cow? Once you have a firm grasp of those weak areas, be methodical and work on them in practice. Don't be discouraged

"Try to cut cows and hold them longer than anyone else."

Kobie Wood

by your weaknesses—go for the throat to overcome them.

Many things happen spontaneously during a cutting run. Sometimes it seems difficult to isolate skills and decide what areas need to be worked on first. But there are key skills that will wreak havoc in your cutting when they are weak, such as stabilizing your center of balance, having a plan in the herd, and riding your horse for position as you work the cow.

Identify your weakest areas and create a cutting program designed to boost the confidence levels of both you and your horse. Then, in order to improve, practice and focus on those weak areas consistently. Without preparing yourself thoroughly, you enter the show arena feeling vulnerable. If you have done all that you can do to prepare yourself mentally, emotionally, and technically prior to competition, you will go into the arena feeling confident.

Prepare Your Horse

The same ideas described above apply to your horse. Concentrate on your horse's weakest areas to make sure he is prepared physically, mentally, and technically. It's imperative that your horse be in prime physical condition. It's unfair and can cause your horse physical pain and injury if you pull him out of the pasture to show on weekends without having him thoroughly conditioned.

Condition Your Horse Physically

I prefer interval aerobic exercises to get—and keep—my horses in shape. Interval aerobics raises and lowers heart-rate

Pre-Show Preparation

I maintain my horse's peak physical condition by walking, trotting, and loping at least three times a week. If I'm showing a more high-strung horse who needs a lot of warming up on the day of the show, I like to begin getting him down at home two or three days prior to the event. This reduces his energy level on a gradual basis and isn't as hard on his body on show day.

levels over time as opposed to linear aerobic exercise which keeps those levels static. For example, if your conditioning program consists of walking your horse for a few minutes then loping for 20 minutes with no breaks, you are practicing linear aerobics. However, if your conditioning program involves walking your horse five minutes, trotting 10 minutes, walking five minutes, loping 10 minutes, walking seven or eight minutes (going the other direction), trotting 10 minutes, walking five minutes, loping 10 minutes, you are utilizing interval aerobic training.

I first became aware of interval aerobic training at LGE Sport Science. It's a part of the basic conditioning program for all LGE athletes. It toughens a person (and, I believe, a horse) physically, mentally, and emotionally. It also promotes relaxation and focus.

Prepare Your Horse Technically

Design a preparation program to make sure your horse is tuned up and ready prior to a show. Some horses will perform better at the show if they have been worked on cattle once during the week, while others need three or four days of practice. The real challenge for non-pros lies in balancing your horse's training needs with your own riding needs during practice. Consider your needs, your horse's needs, and find a balance that works for both.

Preparation on the Day of the Show

On show day, your focus should be on your job. Now that you have done your homework before the show, get yourself ready, get

"Dream it and then do it. A competitive person is forever re-evolving themselves."

Joe Heim

your horse ready, and show with authority during each moment of your two and one-half minute run. That is simply all your job involves. It's easy, however, to get bogged down in fears and what-ifs and lose sight of your job. Prior to making your run, there are five steps to help bring everything together during your run.

Step #1:   *The Warm-Up*

The warm-up involves getting yourself and your horse mentally and physically prepared to show. Exercise your horse so that his energy level is calm yet alert and ready. Too much trotting and loping and your horse is fatigued . . . too little and he's too fresh. Experiment to discover what your horse needs. Always stay tuned in to his body language and behavior instead of going with a regimented and timed exercise plan.

I like to plan my horse's warm-up so that it coincides with getting myself ready. I take several things into consideration to accomplish this. First, I plan how long I think it will take to get my horse down. Then, I give myself extra time in case something unexpected comes up. I also like to watch at least one or two bunches of cattle so that I can get an idea of the kind of cattle at that show on that particular day. Since my horse's warm-up is integrated with my watching cattle, I often have to arrive at the cutting extra early to do some of the horse's warm-up prior to the start of the cutting.

To mentally prepare myself while I trot or lope my horse, I review my job by going through my run, step by step, and remind myself to stay focused. And, even though it's often difficult to

Once the draw is announced, the next step is to plan your herdwork strategy. Do you cut for shape only or do you choose to combine cutting specific cattle with cutting for shape?

remember to drink plenty of water at a show, it's an important part of staying focused. Likewise, eating every couple of hours will ensure that your blood-sugar levels stay intact.

Once I have my horse down, I maintain that energy level by alternately walking and long trotting. (I prefer to long trot because it exercises the horse more evenly.) Make certain you do not allow your horse to freshen up by only walking him (or worse yet, tying him up) the last 30 to 45 minutes before you show.

The warm-up is a critical part of showing. It's a balancing act to meet your mental and physical needs as well as those of your horse. Prepare yourself and your horse to be ready to go when it's your turn.

Step #2: *A Herdwork Plan*

Once the draw is announced, the next step is to plan your herdwork strategy. Do you cut for shape only or do you choose to combine cutting specific cattle with cutting for shape? No matter which approach you choose, it is important to know the bad cattle. Refer to Chapters Eight and Nine for an in-depth discussion on describing cattle and predicting their behavior.

Ideally, I like to get my horse ready and then have someone else walk and trot him so that I can study the cattle before my turn. When that's not an option, I get my horse thoroughly prepared just prior to the time when my cattle enter the arena. Then, during the cattle settling, I concentrate to observe the best and worst cattle. As cutters before me make their cuts, I watch how cattle drive to

Ask your helpers to help you <u>before</u> your class. If you like,
ask them if they would help you study cattle. But remember
that you need to study the cattle yourself and be responsible
for your own cow decisions.

the center of the arena and then return to the back fence during the cuts. I also watch how specific cattle act behind the cutter while he is cutting. When the cutter is working his last cow, I'll begin trotting and continue to walk and/or trot between turns until the next cutter begins his cut. Then, I'll stop and begin to concentrate on cattle again. This way I can watch cattle and maintain my horse's readiness at the same time.

Step #3:   *Communication With Your Helpers*

Line up your helpers before your class. If you like, ask them if they would help you study cattle. But always remember that while people may be more than willing to help you watch cattle, most don't feel comfortable with the sole responsibility of studying cattle for you. You need to be responsible for your own destiny and study the cattle yourself. Then, both you and your helpers can compare choices prior to your run. If you are a new cutter, certainly you can rely on a trainer or your friends to help with cattle selection. However, the only way to gain experience studying the herd is to practice and gradually evolve into a partnership with your help, knowing that during your run you hold the reins and are totally responsible for your decisions. You can always ask for help, but don't turn that job over to someone else without putting forth your own effort.

Have you ever felt distracted or confused when all your helpers talk at one time or say conflicting things to you during your run? One solution is to communicate with your help and design a

Showmanship Poise

If you have a choice between quitting a cow on the fence or quitting a cow in the center of the arena, quit in the center. Your run presentation will be enhanced by the amount of courage and poise shown by bringing the cow off the fence and back to the center of the arena.

system so that what they say during your run helps—not hinders—you. Begin by telling them you go into the ozone when everyone talks at once! Place the blame on your shoulders, not theirs. At the same time, mention that you would like each one of them to have their own focus. For example, one helper can locate cattle while another is in charge of telling you to step up during the cut while still another reminds you to stay relaxed as you work the cow. With this approach, each person can truly help you by saying or doing what's most meaningful to you.

Sometimes non-pros think, "Who am I to give suggestions to my helpers?" As a matter of good communication, I suggest that you approach helpers by seeking out their advice first and then offering your ideas. A great way to discuss cattle is to ask, "What do you think of the yellow, horned cow?" Wait for their response and then state your opinion. Although the advice you receive may not be exactly what you were thinking, that's okay. Exchange ideas and develop your plan from there.

The next time you go to a cutting, look around and notice who is helping. Chances are it's the same group of people run after run, class after class. Some cutters just assume that those same people will be their helpers. If you say "Hey Joe, just stay there" prior to your run, Joe will probably be happy to help you but may not be tuned into you and your horse's particular needs and desires. Set yourself apart by communicating with your helpers during the cattle change before your class. Discuss particulars like your cattle

Rituals anchor you and your horse into a focused,
energized state of mind and body just before
riding to the herd.

plan, and express how much you rely on, and appreciate, their help. You can also *show* them how much you appreciate their help. For example, bring them something to drink or water their turnback horse during the cattle changes. By being sincerely appreciative, you build rapport with four helpers who will go the extra mile for you during your run.

Step #4: *Rituals*

Although the importance of rituals was discussed in detail in Chapter Five, it is re-emphasized here because it is a vital part of preparation prior to your run. It anchors you and your horse into a focused, energized state of mind and body just before riding to the herd. Prepare your horse and prepare yourself by creating a ritual that you perform every time you get ready to show.

Step #5: *The First Impression*

From the moment the judge sees you enter the arena (whether you are still completing your ritual or walking toward the herd), you're making an impression. Although it's not part of the official judging time, be aware that you're presenting an image to the judge. I suggest that you portray confidence in your posture and finesse in the preparation of your horse.

Outstanding Run Presentation Skills

Flexible Herdwork

All the pieces of great herdwork (entering the herd, driving out, making the cut) initiate your run. Whether cutting for shape or

Stay flexible in your herdwork.

Analytical thinking happens as you enter the herd, make the turn and step up towards the center of the arena.

Instinctive thinking takes over as the cut unfolds.

cutting specific cattle, be clear about your plan and let your helpers know what that plan is. As you approach the herd with a take-charge attitude, stay cool, aware, and responsive to what is actually happening in front of you because an important aspect of success-ful showing is being flexible. If you end up cutting a cow that is not the ideal cow, no problem. Just stay offensive, maintain a look of control, and quit at the first opportunity. In your herdwork and while working a cow, you want to give the impression that you love everything that happens! If you find yourself in precarious situations, maintain a confident look on the outside.

Another aspect of herdwork is understanding how to think while you make your cut. The process combines analytical think-ing with instinctive decisions. Analytical thinking happens during the beginning of the cut as you enter the herd, make the turn towards the center of the arena, and step up. You can continue to think analytically as your eyes scan, gaining information about the cattle in front of you and how the situation is developing. In the beginning, as you enter the herd, for example, you might be think-ing, "There's the black baldy, the yellow mott, and the redneck. The black mott is in the best spot to be cut now. I'll step to her." Of course, all this occurs in a matter of moments. Then, as you step towards a certain cow you might make an instant decision about how the cow reacted. You either continue with your original plan or switch to cutting for shape. Things at this point happen in micro-seconds. No matter how quickly these decisions are made,

"You want to paint a pretty picture. It's important to look professional. Be cautious and know the herd well enough so that when your help makes suggestions, you know whether their advice is good or not. Also, knowing what kind of cow your horse works best may be something your help doesn't know. Bottom line: Think for yourself."

Ronnie Nettles

when you're feeling calm and focused, it doesn't feel rushed.

Thinking instinctively takes over as the situation continues to unfold—especially when things speed up or your plan isn't happening! Trusting your instincts comes from experience and from telling yourself to stay cool and see what actually happens, moment to moment.

Don't forget to rely on your acting skills for the cut—shoulders back, chin up, eyes forward—as you walk to and through the herd. Then, once you take charge of your cow on the cut and put your hand down on your horse's neck, your body shifts, physiologically. You go into a "working the cow" mode—a more slumped physical position and an instinctive mental process. Your hand is down, your eyes are on the cow, and your lower back is rounded. Thinking is purely automatic.

Working the Cow

What separates experienced, successful cutters from less experienced cutters is their ability to be responsive to their horse and to the situation, moment to moment. A great show person can shift gears to help his horse, especially when errors occur—the horse is too long, the horse falls back toward the herd, the horse doesn't stop completely. He knows that one of the main skills of showing is to be instantly responsive. While it is natural to get anxious when things get out of whack, that reaction blocks your ability to perform at your best. Mental tension produces a physical response (muscles tighten, legs grip, heels come up, heart rate

For the entire time—from the time you drop your hand until you quit a cow—stay aggressive to hold your line with the cow when possible and stay alive by riding your horse until the moment you quit.

increases, brain wave activity increases). It may help you to relax, enjoy, and even welcome the challenge of riding responsively, moment to moment, by realizing that no horse is ever perfect. They all need us to help them. The great, successful riders maintain a cool aggressiveness. They stay responsive to their own emotions, their horse, or the cattle.

For the entire time—from the time you drop your hand until you quit a cow—stay aggressive to hold your line with the cow when possible, and stay alive by riding your horse until the moment you quit. Be gritty, cool, and offensive.

Quitting a Cow

Good cattle actually have about 15 to 30 seconds of excellent "working life." Working life means showing interest in the horse and wanting to get back into the herd, but not too aggressively. An ideal cow moves 15 to 40 feet at medium speed and consistently stops and turns toward the cutter. Once a cow's behavior changes and they begin to run from fence to fence, get very aggressive in returning to the herd, or run toward the turnback area, more often than not they will not become a "good" cow again and become interested in your horse. Unless there is some special circumstance—only a few seconds left and you want to be working the cow at the buzzer—it is time to quit and get another cow. In the ideal scenario, find an opportunity to quit the cow in the center of the arena as it conveys an image of finesse and control to the judge. With experience, you will begin to "read" a cow and spot

How To Acquire the Free-Flowing, Instinctive State of Great Showmen

1. **Use images to keep your riding automatic.** Mentally feel how it is to make a beautiful cut instead of being too analytical about it. Images are powerful and work by automatically programming your mind and body for success.

2. **Work on rhythm and tempo to smooth mechanics.** Working a cow is rhythmic. Sometimes counting or mentally repeating a rhythmic tune or a phrase can re-establish flow.

3. **Steady your breathing.** Become aware of your breathing and simply let the air flow in and out of your abdomen whenever possible. Try exhaling when you see the cow begin to stop and always breathe between cattle.

4. **Use some mental cues instead of analysis to remember what you've planned.** Come up with a phrase that will trigger the moves you need. For example, "look at the top," "stay aggressive." "eyes up."

5. **Set up rituals.** Relax for one or two seconds between cattle. Then review your plan. This simple ritual will help you stay focused, instinctive, and let go of mistakes. You'll look positively to the next move.

when her point-earning time is about to expire. You'll also be able to make decisions about waiting for an opportunity to quit in the center of the arena or quitting whenever the opportunity presents itself.

Of course, some cattle you cut will not be good. If there is an immediate threat of losing it, quit at your first opportunity. A mark of showmanship is learning when to quit a bad cow quickly and go back into the herd for another. In other situations, where cattle are generally terrible, survival may be the name of the game. You might be happy to find even one cow that will stay in front of you and run wall to wall! Suddenly, she's the "good cow." It's all relative to the herd and the day's situation. It's about making the best decisions to maximize your horse's potential given a particular set of circumstances.

Between Cattle

LGE's Mentally Tough training has made me keenly aware that what happens between cattle is critical to your ability to put together great, consistent runs. The specific tools I share with you here are used by professional and Olympic athletes to maintain high performance levels throughout their performance time. Once I began applying these techniques to my own showing, I experienced a sense of planned mental and emotional control. Utilize these strategies and you will stop making radical, panicky decisions that are so easy to do in cutting.

The strategy involves a specific four-part process between

No matter how hairy things were while working the cow, quit with finesse. Smoothly pick your rein hand up and place your opposite hand on your horse's neck. All the while, keep your eyes on the cow. Maintain a look of total control.

cattle which allows you to maintain physical control, relax, plan, and get back into action on the next cow—all within a 10 to 20 second window of time. In other sports (except timed events), after significant action has occurred, there is a small window of time that offers a natural break in the action. In baseball, it is between pitches. In tennis, it is between points. In cutting, it is between cattle. Dr. James Loehr of LGE Sport Science, Inc. believes it is critically important to specifically train and discipline yourself to execute these four steps at planned times during your event.

Part #1:   *Positive Physical Response*

The first step is to respond positively to what has already occurred in your run, no matter what actually happened, positive or negative. The reason that a positive physical response is so important is because when you act with poise on the outside, you stay clear and focused on the inside. In cutting, part one begins by quitting the cow smoothly. No matter how hairy the quit may have seemed, pick your rein hand up and place your opposite hand on your horse's neck. All the while keep your eyes on the cow. If you look at the cow for a few moments after the quit, the control of your eyes will slow your mind. It also helps give you and your horse a look of control and confidence. Then, as you turn toward the herd, move fluidly, smoothly, and calmly.

The next time you go to a cutting, observe how others quit their cattle. Notice how frantic hand motions, looking down at the

"Try to cut a cow that will show your horse. Do not over show."

Jack Newton

ground, and wheeling a horse back toward the herd projects a feeling of anxiousness. Then observe the opposite. Responding positively with your body at the beginning of the quit to initiate this time between cattle is not a question of right or wrong. It is a matter of presenting a look of finesse and poise while, at the same time, maintaining mental and emotional control within.

Part #2: *Recovery*

In cutting, the recovery period happens following your smooth quit. It begins after you turn toward the herd and just before you re-enter the herd. As you face the herd, pause momentarily. Completely relax and take a deep breath. If it helps, tell yourself that "everything's okay" or simply, "relax." The recovery process alters your physiology as muscle tension is reduced, your heart rate is slowed, and your brain-wave patterns become rhythmic again. A sense of calmness allows you to think, continue your herdwork plan, and decide how aggressive to be on this cut depending on what you have accomplished so far. To be able to truly relax during this one- to three-second time frame, you must condition this skill at home. I suggest that between cattle at home, you stop, breathe, and wait (no matter how long it takes) until you feel yourself relax and your body chemistry changes. It's wonderful training for your horse, too.

Part #3: *Planning*

During this time, evaluate what you have done so far in your run and determine what you need to do next i.e., which cow to cut,

Before you re-enter
the herd, evaluate
what you have done
so far in your run and
determine what you
need to do next.

Make a commitment
to drive up, cut clean,
and make your cut in
the middle of the
arena. Step up
coolly, but
aggressively.

how aggressive to be, and how much risk to take to build your run. Great cutters have this planning ability honed to such a high degree that it is second nature for them to reflect on what has happened and determine their next step.

Part #4:   *Take Charge to Make the Cut*

The last step of this four-part process is a commitment to drive up, cut clean, and make your cut in the middle of the arena. Step up coolly but aggressively. Make your cut to present you and your horse with confidence and build your run.

These four distinct stages of what you do between cattle allow you to present you and your horse with finesse and maintain mental and emotional control. Although these four parts occur within 10 to 20 seconds, the clarity of practicing each part and then combining them is a powerful and effective process.

Spontaneous Responses to Unexpected Situations

One of the most frustrating things about cutting is the lack of control over unexpected situations that arise during your run. Great cutters have the ability to be responsive, moment to moment, to the situation at hand and respond with the best possible action. It is a sure bet that sometime, somewhere you will run into one or all of the following:

1. Cow running out

2. Gates opening/fences falling

3. Helper not showing up or having problems with his horse

National Cutting Horse Association Official Handbook of Rules and Regulations

The NCHA rule book contains the most in-depth information anywhere regarding the guidelines and rules which govern the showing and judging of a cutting horse. The rule book is available through the NCHA headquarters located in Fort Worth, Texas. I recommend that you take special note of the following sections:

1. Rules for Judging Cutting Horse Contests
2. Self-Adjusted Monitor System
3. Some Points on Showing and Judging the Cutting Horse
4. Judging Casebook
5. Non-Professional Casebook

4. Bridle falling off or rein breaking

5. Loud noises scaring your horse or the cattle

My most generic advice is to let your acting skills kick in. Show no negative emotion on the outside and stay focused on your job. Whether you survive the situation or not, know that this is a part of cutting. Let go, don't resist the uncontrollable and look ahead to your next run.

Enjoy experimenting with the suggestions in this chapter, while developing your own showmanship style. Trust yourself and your horse and let it happen as you project confidence. And, no matter what happens, keep cutting fun. There will always be another cutting.

And now, some final words for you in the Afterword.

AFTERWORD

For as long as your passion for cutting continues, there's more—more to learn, more new friends, more room to grow in self-discovery, more horses, more fun, more exciting runs to grin about, more runs to cry about. It's a way of life that reaches the very depths of our souls.

I wish you a lifetime of fun and harmony within yourself and with your horse as you continue to learn. Always, always, believe in yourself.

RESOURCES

CUTTING

Videos:

Approaches to Cutting . . . . Bill Freeman
Cutting Fundamentals . . . . Al Dunning
Cutting, Just the Basics . . . . Bill Riddle
Mentally Tough Cutting . . . . Barbra Schulte
Herd Management Skills . . . . Barbra Schulte
Physical & Behavioral Characteristics
   of Cattle . . . . Barbra Schulte
Competition Cutting . . . . Bill Freeman
Cutting Clinic . . . . Joe Heim
NCHA Futurities 1987-1997 . . . . NCHA
Legends of Cutting . . . . Red Steagall

Books:

Cutting . . . . Leon Harrel
Cutting: A Guide for the Non-Pro
   Competitor . . . . Sally Harrison
Cutting: Training the Horse and Rider . . . . Bill Freeman
                                              with Gala Nettles
Cutting, First the Basics . . . . Bill Riddle
Doc Bar . . . . Gala Nettles
Just Shorty . . . . Gala Nettles
King Ranch and Little Peppy: The Legend and
   the Legacy . . . . Gala Nettles
Mr. Pat . . . . Gala Nettles
Pride in the Dust . . . . Don Weller
Training and Showing the Cutting Horse . . . . . Lynn Champion
NCHA Official Handbook of Rules and Regulations . . . NCHA

Publications:
The Cutting Horse Chatter . . . . Ft. Worth, TX
America's Cutter . . . . Terrel, TX
ACHA Cuttin' Review . . . . Ft. Worth, TX

Organizations:
NCHA - National Cutting Horse Association
260 Bailey Avenue
Ft. Worth, TX 76107-1862 817-244-6188
ACHA - American Cutting Horse Association
P.O. Box 2443
Brenham, TX 77834 979-836-3370

MENTALLY TOUGH

Books:
Mental Toughness Training . . . . Jim Loehr, Ed. D.
The New Toughness Training for Sports . . . . Jim Loehr, Ed. D.
Stress for Success . . . . Jim Loehr, Ed. D.
Toughness Training for Life . . . . Jim Loehr, Ed. D.
The Mental Game . . . . Jim Loehr, Ed. D.

Audio:
Love the Battle . . . . Jim Loehr, Ed. D.
The Get Tough Tape . . . . Jim Loehr, Ed. D.
Mentally Tough Formula for Maximum Performance
. . . . Jim Loehr, Ed. D.
Mentally Tough 16 Tape Training System . . Jim Loehr, Ed. D.
and Jack Groppel, Ph. D., F.A.C.S.M.

BIOGRAPHY OF CUTTERS
who have contributed quotes to this book

Keith Barnett

Keith has been in the cutting industry for 35 years as a trainer, teacher, and showman. Keith is a member of the NCHA Executive Board. He rode the 1987 NCHA Open World Champion Gelding, has been a NCHA Top Ten Finalist 15 times, and is a member of the NCHA Riders Hall of Fame. Keith feels his success is a result of hard work. His favorite horses include Short Doc, McKay Alice, Duece Five, Big Red Solano, Colonel Flip, and Taris Catalyst.

Sandy Bonelli

Sandy has been in the cutting industry for 20 years. She breeds, raises, trains, and shows her own cutting horses. Her career highlights include 1984, 1987 and 1998 NCHA Super Stakes Non-Pro Champion, 1989 and 1997 NCHA Futurity Non-Pro Champion, 1995 Super Stakes Open Champion and 1998 NCHA Derby Open Champion. Sandy attributes her success to her mother and father, Kathy Daughn, Faron Hightower, Chubby Turner, and Tom Lyons. She also credits many friends for their support through good times and bad. Favorite horses of Sandy's include Shakin Flo, Smart Little Rondee, Oakalola, Bella Coquette, and A Little Starlight.

Kathy Boone

The daughter of famed cutting horse trainer and sculptor Jim Reno, Kathy has been in the cutting industry her entire life. In 1991 and 1995, Kathy was the NCHA Non-Pro Reserve World Champion and was inducted into the NCHA Hall of Fame in 1994. She owes her success to the support of her entire family. Two of Kathy's favorite horses are Chicks Playboy and Smart Peppy Lena.

Millie Kay Bouget

Millie has been in the cutting industry since she was 4 years old. She began her showing career as a youth competitor. Millie Kay was the NCHA Youth World Champion in 1988 and 1990 and the NCHA Youth World Reserve Champion in 1991, 1992, and 1993. She was also the 1988 NCHA $10,000 Non-Pro World Champion. Mille Kay attributes her success to her parents. "My father trained and hauled me up and down the road and guided me in the right direction. My mother stuck by me the whole way and was there when I needed a Mom." Favorite horses of Millie Kay's include Smoke On Echols, Rio Panchita, SR Joses Joy, Little Smarty Chex, Especials Lady, Haida Partner, and Dual Fun Time.

Lindy Burch

Lindy has been in the cutting horse industry for 25 years as a trainer, breeder, and showman. She was the 1979 NCHA Futurity Open Reserve Champion and the 1980 NCHA Futurity Open Champion. In 1980 she was the PCCHA, OCHA, and NWCHA Futurity Champion riding three different horses. Lindy was also the 1993 Masters Reserve Champion and won the 1995 and 1997 NCHA World Championship Open Finals. She says her success is based on a combination of great horses, hard work and lots of luck. Favorite horses of Lindy's include Diamond Mystery, Miss Royal Mahogany, Royal Red Boon, Bet Yer Blue Boon's, Shesa Smarty Lena, Dry Doc Dottie, Bunny Starlight, and Scarlet O'Lena.

Dick Cogdell

Dick has been in the cutting industry for 25 years as an owner, breeder, and showman. He is a director of the local NCHA affiliate. He won the 1993 NCHA Derby Non-Pro Championship and was the 1994 Augusta Futurity Classic Non-Pro Champion. Dick attributes his success to his father, Billy Cogdell. Favorite horses of Dick's include Susie Dry, Rattlesnake Jones, Swingin, and San Peppy's Miss.

Mitch Farris

Mitch has been involved in the cutting industry over 20 years. In 1984, Mitch earned distinction as the NCHA Non-Pro Reserve World Champion. He was a Top Ten Non-Pro from 1983 to 1989. Mitch attributes his success to his parents' support and encouragement and also to Gold Pardon. His favorite horses include Gold Pardon, Willys Tivio Babe, and Peppy La Pu. Mitch has a four-year-old son, named Kyle, and teaches Jr. High Science.

Phil Feinberg

Phil has been in the cutting industry since 1978. He is a member of the NCHA Non-Pro Hall of Fame. In 1984, he earned the title as the PCCHA Non-Pro Year-End Champion. Phil attributes his success to Gary Bellenfant, Ray Hunt, Crawford Hall, Greg Ward, Dave MacGregor, Chubby Turner, Faron Hightower, and Richard Anderson. His favorite horses include Little Orphan Lena, Montana Doc, Docs Otoetta, Jae Bar Fletch, Bob Acre Doc, and Docs Starlight.

Dick Gaines

Dick has been in the cutting industry since 1978. He is a trainer, breeder, and showman in aged events and weekend cuttings. He is also a member of the NCHA Riders Hall of Fame and the NCHA Non-Pro Hall of Fame. He owes much of his success to Gayle Borland, Shorty Freeman, Buster Welch and many others. "I have never asked for help from a cutter and *not* received it." His favorite horses include Zack T Wood and Lintons Lady Doc.

Lee Garner

Lee has been involved in the cutting industry for 10 years as a breeder and showman. In 1989, Lee was the Congress Open Champion. In 1990, he was the Non-Pro World Champion and in 1996 he was the NCHA Futurity Non-Pro Champion. Lee owes his success to his family for their support, his wife Kathy, the grace of God, the support of friends Norman Burton and Elbert Sides, and Baldy Freckles, one of Lee's favorite horses. Peopnitas Acre is another favorite horse. "They have proved they can work through a handicap—me!"

Helen Groves

Helen has been involved with horses that work cattle since her childhood on the legendary King Ranch. Helen raises and shows home-bred champions like Imari Tari, Haida's Dude, and Haida's Lori. She has also served as president of local cutting affiliates. She is a NCHA Director and Director Emeritus of the United States Equestrian Team. Helen attributes her success to good horses and good trainers, including Buster Welch, John Carter, Red Stevenson, Wray Crabtree, Willie Richardson, June Mitchell, Rodney Schumann, Josh King, Cindy Adams, Beth Byerly, Mike Mowery, Gary Bellenfant, Greg Welch, and Grady Duncan. "I can't name them all!" Helen gives a special thanks to her parents, Bob and Helen Kleberg for bringing her up with horses, her children for keeping her going, and all of her cutting friends—pro and non-pro—who have befriended and helped her all these years. Favorite horses of Helen's include Miss Peppy Also and Imari Tari.

Paul Hansma

Paul has been in the cutting industry since 1984. He serves as chairman of the NCHA Limited Aged Event Committee. Paul has been a finalist and/or champion in multiple NCHA aged events, including the NCHA Open Futurity Champion in 1996. In 1994, he won NCHA Horse of the Year with Hicapoo. Paul is also a member of the NCHA Hall of Fame. He attributes his success to a solid upbringing and good horses. Paul's favorite horses are those at the top of their events. He enjoys a good horse whether it's a ranch, show, or kid's horse.

Winston Hansma

Winston began riding cutting horses in 1983 with Charlie Ward on the Doc Bar Ranch. He is a trainer and manager of the Bar H Ranche, which has a program dedicated to the improvement and promotion of the cutting horse. In 1994, Winston was the NCHA Open Futurity Champion, and he was the NCHA Derby Open Champion in 1993, 1995 and 1997. He owes his success to the unselfish support system at the Bar H Ranche and to Danny Motes, who convinced him to believe in himself. Favorite horses of Winston's include CD Olena, Smokin Dually, and Dually Lena. Winston feels fortunate to be involved in a career that is a constant challenge, allowing him to look forward to the start of each day.

Spencer Harden

Spencer began his cutting career in 1958. He breeds, raises, trains, and shows. In 1989 he was the NCHA Open Futurity Champion. He is a three-time Non-Pro Futurity Champion and a five-time Non-Pro Reserve Futurity Champion. He attributes his success to love and dedication to the sport. Spencer's favorite horses include Bill's Jazabell, Hickoryote, Jazabell Quixote, July Jazz, and Wee Darlin.

Bobby Hawkins

Bobby has been in the cutting industry for 18 years. He shows in limited aged events and weekend cuttings and is involved as a breeder. In 1989 he won the Non-Pro Challenge and in 1990 he was the 1990 AQHA Amateur World Champion. He owes his success to his wife, Georgette, and to Don Parker's expertise on cutting. Bobby's favorite horses include Athena Peppy, Sassy Diamond Doc, and Tinas Little Peppy.

Joe Heim

Joe has been in the cutting industry for 25 years as a breeder and trainer. In 1983, Joe and Docs Okie Quiote won the NCHA Open Futurity Championship. In 1984, they won the NCHA Super Stakes and NCHA Derby to claim a remarkable triple-crown. Joe attributes his success to good luck and hard work. "The harder I've worked, the more luck I've had." His favorite horses are the ones that have won money.

James Hooper

James has been in the cutting horse industry for 17 years as a breeder, owner, and non-pro rider showing in limited aged events and weekend shows. James has made the finals in numerous limited-aged shows and served a two-year term as president of the NCHA. He attributes his success to persistence, a competitive nature, and the support of his fellow cutters. Favorite horses of James include Lenas O Lady and every horse that makes the finals.

Dan Lufkin

Dan has been involved in the cutting industry since 1978. He has enjoyed breeding, training, showing, and selling cutting horses. Dan has been champion or reserve champion in numerous limited aged events. He is a member of the NCHA Hall of Fame. His success is a result of long hours in the saddle and hard work. Favorite horses of Dan's include Scarlet O'Lena and Lena's Louella.

Mary Jo Milner

Mary Jo has been in the cutting industry for 20 years. She is a two-time NCHA Non-Pro World Champion. Mary Jo attributes her success to prayer. Her favorite horses include Docs Becky and Playboys Kid.

Ronnie Nettles

Ronnie has been in the cutting industry for 38 years. Beyond training for the public, breeding and judging, Ronnie is the designer of Nettles Stirrups and the owner of Nettles Stirrup Manufacturing Co. He was the 1984 NCHA Futurity Champion, the 1985 NCHA Super Stakes Champion, and the 1989 NCHA Derby Co-Reserve Champion. Ronnie is a member of the NCHA Hall of Fame and has won the AQHA World Reserve Championship. Dedication, hard work, and family support are Ronnie's keys to success. His favorite horses include Doc Per, Personality Doc, Cash Quioxte Playboy, and Sancie Playgirl.

Jack Newton

Jack has been involved in the cutting industry for 50 years and is a founding member of the NCHA. He has served as a NCHA director and as a member of the Executive Board. Jack is a member of the NCHA Hall of Fame. In 1959, he was the NCHA Open World Champion. He attributes his success to hard work and the opportunity to ride good horses. Jack's favorite horses include Poco Stampede, Swen Miss 16, Commander King, and Hollywood Bill.

John Paxton

John has been involved in the cutting industry for 30 years as an owner, exhibitor, and judge. In 1982, he was the NCHA Non-Pro World Champion and the NCHA Five-Year-Old Classic Open Champion. John attributes his success to Jimmy Orrell, Wray Crabtree, Terry Riddle, Bill Riddle, and his father, Albert Paxton, for allowing him to learn to lose and learn to work hard enough to overcome losing. His favorite horses include Docs Otoetta, Hollywood Boy, Docs Tlingit, and Docs Tin Lizzie.

Gil Porter

Gil has been involved in the cutting industry for 33 years as a rider, breeder, and judge. He is a NCHA Director and has served as president of his local affiliate on several occasions. Gil says he attributes his success to the people who help at shows. Some of his favorite horses include War China, Miss China Cat, Chopstick, Vandalano, Mr. China Cat, and Mickey Dawson. "Cutting is a disease for which there is no cure."

Corky Sokol

Corky has been involved in the cutting industry since 1980. He is a NCHA Top Ten Rider and the 1988 NCHA Derby Open Reserve Champion. Corky is also a past Open Champion of the National Championships in Jackson, Mississippi. Favorite horses include Colonel Bar Glo, Jae Bar Mina, Handle Bar Jane, Gay Handle Jane, Sons Miss Sprat, Special Kory, Peppys Tachita, and Jae Bar Sonya.

Gene Suiter

Gene has been involved in the cutting industry since 1961. He has conducted both training and judging clinics and has had approximately 25 years of combined service on both the Pacific Coast and the NCHA Board of Directors. Gene was the NCHA Futurity Reserve Champion twice, the Pacific Coast Futurity Champion twice and past Champion of the Pacific Coast 4-year-old, 5-year-old, 6-year-old, 7-up, Cutting Stakes and Gelding Stakes. He has been in the NCHA Top Ten several times. He is also a member of the NCHA Hall of Fame. Gene owes his success to Buster Welch. Favorite horses of his include Jose Uno, Callans Man, Montana Doc, and Docs Gunsmoke.

Carole Thorsnes

Carole has been involved in the cutting industry for 14 years. Carole's biggest win was the 1991 NCHA Futurity Non-Pro and $50,000 Amateur. She has also won the 4-year-old Non-Pro Championship in Reno, Nevada. Carole owes her success to Rod Kelley and his training. Her favorite horses include SR Hyacinth, SR Gata, and Mary Jo Lena.

Kobie Wood

Kobie has been a professional trainer since 1981 when he turned in his non-pro card. His interests include breeding, training, showing, and sales. In 1990, Kobie was the NCHA Open World Champion riding Cash Quioxte Rio. "Cash Quioxte Rio showed me that I could accomplish my dreams." In 1995 and 1997, Kobie was NCHA Open World Champion riding Meradas Little Sue. In 1992, he was the NCHA Open Derby Reserve Champion. Kobie owes his success to his father L.H. Wood for having faith in his training. Favorite horses of Kobie's include Wyoming Doc, Tari Chick Gay, Chickasha an Tari, Tari Rey Gay, Cash Quioxte Rio, Red White and Boon, Smart War Lena, Chicks Playboy, Meradas Little Sue, Duals Blue Boon, Chita Cash, Pappions Cat, Boons Bar Gold, and Brian King.

L.H. Wood

L.H. has been in the cutting horse industry for 44 years as a breeder, trainer, teacher, and judge. He serves as a director of the NCHA. In 1985, he was the Non-Pro Co-Reserve Champion of the NCHA Futurity. He attributes his success to patience from his wife and family, having well-bred horses, and the training by his son, Kobie. Favorite horses are Chickasha Gay, Flo Doc and Honey Farr. "They say every cowboy is entitled to one good horse, one good dog and one good wife. I've had them all."

BARBRA SCHULTE RESOURCES

Barbra Schulte Cutting Video Series
A three-volume video series. Volume I - *Mentally Tough Cutting* teaches cutters to be calm, focused and aggressive during their cutting run. In Volume II - *Physical and Behavioral Characteristics of Cattle*, discover how to pick the right cow from the herd by developing great cattle watching skills. Understand strategies to gain control in the herd through Volume III - *Herd Management Skills* with seven fundamental herd management skills.

Cutting One Run at a Time
A practical guide to cutting success. This book provides tips on everything from the basics of riding a trained horse, to mastering cattle and herdwork challenges, to building a strong support system, and more.

Mentally Tough Riding Course
An eight-cassette training course with six workbook lessons contained in a 3-ring binder, a book, and a strength conditioning band. This in-depth training course will help riders of all disciplines to stay calm and focused in the face of distractions, learn visualizations skills transform negative emotions into positive ones, prepare for major events, and more!

Riding with Confidence
This single audio cassette gives riders a concise overview of the Mentally Tough Riding program. This tape is excellent to keep high performance training concepts at your fingertips. It also gives you a convenient and inexpensive way to introduce Mentally Tough training to other riders.

Coaching for Confidence
People who coach other riders often find themselves saying or doing things which actually weaken their attempts to help. This single audio cassette introduces the Mentally Tough philosophies to anyone who is a support person to a rider. Side 1 summarizes key strategies while Side 2 gives you concrete suggestions to help anyone achieve their full potential.

PRODUCT ORDER FORM

For further information or to order products,
fill out the information below or contact us.

Barbra Schulte
Center for Equestrian Performance
2000 S. Market Street, Suite 219
Brenham, TX 77833
979-277-9344
info@barbraschulte.com
www.barbraschulte.com

Name_____

Address_____

City, ST, Zip _____

Phone _____ Fax _____ E-Mail_____

❏ Visa   ❏ Mastercard   ❏ AMX   ❏ Check   ❏ Money order

#_____ exp. _____

❏ Barbra Schulte Cutting Video Series .... $179.95 plus $9.00 S/H _____
❏ Cutting One Run at a Time .... $26.95 plus $7.00 S/H _____
❏ Mentally Tough Riding Course .... $139.95 plus $14.00 S/H _____
❏ Riding with Confidence .... $14.95 plus $4.00 S/H _____
❏ Coaching for Confidence .... $14.95 plus $4.00 S/H _____
TX residents add 8.25% sales tax _____
Shipping/Handling _____
TOTAL _____

Barbra Schulte
2000 S. Market St., Suite 219
Brenham, TX 77833